Triumph Bonneville

Year by Year

Other Titles in the Crowood MotoClassics Series

Triumph Bonneville
Year By Year

Paul Hazeldine

The Crowood Press

First published in 2002 by
The Crowood Press Ltd
Ramsbury, Marlborough
Wiltshire SN8 2HR

British Library Cataloguing-in-Publication Data
A catalogue record for this book is available from the British Library.

ISBN 1 86126 513 1

Acknowledgements
Many thanks to the following for their help with my research: Flordeliza T.
Hazeldine, Mike Poynton, John Eastwood, David Kenny, John R. Nelson, Mick
Walker, James Leslie Finney, Dave Norton, Jack Stewart, Dave Lewis, Colin
Craig, Frank Westworth and the editorial staff at *Classic Bike Guide* magazine,
the National Motorcycle Museum.

Typeset by Servis Filmsetting Ltd, Manchester

Printed and bound in Great Britain by Bookcraft, Midsomer Norton

Contents

Preface

Hindsight has proven the Bonneville to be a 'superbike' in the truest sense of the word, perhaps even the very first of the modern superbikes. Within its own production life the Bonneville became a legend and went on to leave a legacy of sporting success that is envied still.

After steady evolutionary development from Edward Turner's 500cc Speed Twin of 1938, the 650 T120 Bonneville emerged in 1959 to become the definitive bike of the 1960s. Under the supervision of Triumph's competent and enthusiastic management, the 'Bonnie' progressed from the already inspired Speed Twin into a production motorcycle that routinely (at least as far as Triumph's publicity department would have it) set world records and achieved world-wide competition success.

Sadly, even as the bike's reputation peaked at the start of the 1970s the fortunes of the Triumph Engineering Company were fading. The previously safe hands of the original management team faltered. Clear foresight dimmed as conflicting demands clouded marketing policy and confounded production schedules. Finally, workers at the Meriden factory became so alienated that they declared a form of industrial independence, a complete inverse of the spirit of co-operation that had enabled the initial production of that living legend, the Triumph Bonneville.

Despite these troubles, the Triumph Bonneville has become an icon and the legend continues. The modern-day Bonneville is a worthy successor to the bike which is fondly remembered by so many people.

1 Origins

The Triumph Cycle Company

After producing its first motorcycle in 1902, followed by two decades of successful trading, in the early twenties the original Triumph Cycle Company, founded by Siegfried Bettmann in 1887, was taking a closer interest in car manufacturing and considering a move away from its motorcycle heritage. Success in motorcar manufacture marked the beginning of the end for motorcycles at the original Triumph Company.

However, despite this the Triumph name has lived on and motorcycles bearing this name continue to be manufactured in the new millennium, although the original manufacturing companies have long since faltered and closed.

The Beginnings

Siegfried Bettmann: the Founder of Triumph

Siegfried Bettmann arrived from Nuremberg, Germany in November 1883 at the age of 21.

Already fluent in French and English after having enjoyed a good education and a period of post-study relaxation in Paris, Siegfried was determined to capitalize on his knowledge. Both his education and affluent gap-year life style had been funded by his father Mayer Bettmann, estate manager to a wealthy Bavarian land-owning family.

Well aware of his good fortune in life so far, Siegfried was determined to apply his education to good effect in business.

Immediately after his arrival in England, Bettmann started work with Kelly and Co. of the Strand, London. They published a popular range of street and commercial directories and employed Siegfried primarily for his linguistic skills. Not one to be easily satisfied, the ambitious young German kept a keen eye open for a position with better prospects. Within months he had moved on to the London branch of the White Sewing Machine Company, where he eventually became the company's representative covering Europe and North Africa.

In 1885, again restless after a year working for White's, Bettmann decided to go into business on

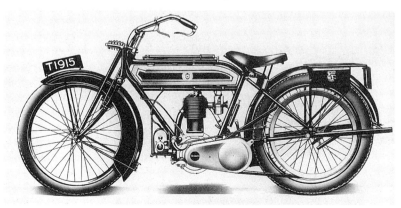

The 1915 Triumph Model H, powered by a 550cc side-valve engine driving a Sturmey-Archer three-speed gearbox through a primary drive chain and clutch. A belt drive completed the transmission. The Model H became a standard mount for British and Allied despatch riders of the Great War.

his own account. He established a trading agency to represent the interests of the handful of German firms who sought business in Britain. One of the more successful clients, in fact the only successful client, was Biesolt and Locke, a sewing machine manufacturer of Meissen in Saxony. On the basis of this single viable company Bettmann's one-man trading agency was founded and somewhat misleadingly named S. Bettmann and Company.

After operating profitably as an import agency trading exclusively in sewing machines, S. Bettmann and Company decided to make the move into exports. Bicycles were gaining respectability as a means of transport and various technical advances were being introduced which made them safer and more easily used by the less expert rider. Bettmann believed that the market for these eminently practical machines would grow. He decided that he and his company could best profit by exporting British-made bicycles to the rest of the European continent.

The Birth of the Triumph Bicycle

The bicycles exported by Bettmann were in fact made by William Andrews, a bicycle manufacturer from Birmingham. Bettmann and Co. merely marketed the machines under its own label without making any mechanical contribution. Although no engineer, Bettmann was a shrewd businessman and he soon recognized that the name 'Bettmann Bicycle' carried little commercial resonance. Instead, the product needed a brand name that would be understood and easily recognized throughout the European market. 'Triumph' met that requirement: assertive, memorable and also, more importantly, easily understood in most of the European countries targeted by Bettmann's export drive.

The name first appeared on export models of the Bettmann bicycle in 1886; one year later, Bettmann and Co. adopted it as the trading title of the company.

During 1887, Mauritz J. Schulte joined the Triumph Cycle Company. Schulte was an engineer who, like Bettmann, came from Germany.

Recognized later as a man of 'great vigour, cool and balanced judgement combined with considerable prudence' Schulte realized that the company could achieve increased profits only by moving into production on its own account. Bettmann agreed with his partner's ideas and in 1889 the Triumph Cycle Company Ltd established a small factory in Earl's Court, off Much Park Street in central Coventry. At that time Coventry was the centre of the bicycle manufacturing industry. With the financial aid of Alderman A.S. Tomson (owner of their rented factory), A.E. Fridlander and other local commercial backers, production of the Triumph bicycle began in earnest.

Bettmann and Schulte's timing was fortunate and useful local business contacts were established through Alderman Tomson and his colleagues. In 1897, Schulte proposed the licensed manufacture of a Hildebrand and Wolfmuller motorcycle and an example of the machine was brought to the Coventry factory for evaluation. Schulte, initially fired with enthusiasm for the project, performed a number of demonstration runs at Coventry Stadium. However the partners ultimately decided that the day of the motorcycle was still to come and for the time being pedal cycle production would remain the company's principal activity. Although originally named and registered as 'New Triumph Company Limited', the title of the business was soon revised to the more descriptive 'Triumph Cycle Company Limited'.

The First Triumph Motorcycle

The first Triumph motorcycle was produced in 1902. This was fitted with an imported Belgian Minerva 239cc engine. This featured an automatic inlet valve and battery-powered coil ignition and, once unleashed, produced $1\frac{3}{4}$hp. In 1903 this was superseded by a side-valve engine from the same manufacturer. During the following year J.A. Prestwich and Belgian Fafnir engines were also made available in Triumph motorcycles.

Triumph Grows and Develops

Significantly, Harvey du Cross, the Dublin-based financier who had backed the obscure veterinary surgeon J.B. Dunlop (later to achieve fame in tyre manufacture) developed a keen interest in the activities of the Triumph Cycle Company.

Bettman was summoned to Dublin where du Cross proposed that, subject to a satisfactory audit of the burgeoning cycle business, the cash-rich Dunlop Tyre Company would make an investment in Triumph. As a result the Triumph Cycle Company's finances were transformed. Financially underwritten by Dunlop and re-capitalized to the tune of £45,000, Triumph's credit rating improved beyond measure. Bettman and Schulte were appointed as joint managing directors of a restructured company now firmly based on secure financial foundations.

With the active encouragement of du Cross, Dunlop company secretary John Griffiths gave up his post to buy carefully selected bicycle shops in order to establish a nationwide cycle dealer network. Griffiths was easily persuaded to take an agency for Triumph's machines and sales increased dramatically. By 1905, Triumph had designed and produced its own 3hp engine and fitted magneto ignition to some models. The old Much Park Street factory was soon unable to meet the growing demand and in 1907 mainstream manufacturing was moved to a new site in Priory Street, Coventry. During the first year at the new factory 1,000 machines were produced, and by 1909 Triumph's output had risen to 3,000 machines per year.

The Triumph Cycle Company was converted into a public company. By any measure the company flotation was a huge success. Available stock was ten times over-subscribed by investors who were anxious to secure a slice of what was now widely recognized as a growth industry. The flotation gave many original Triumph shareholders, some of them personal friends who had backed Bettmann and Schulte in their earliest endeavours, the chance to realize respectable gains.

The Much Park Street site, Bettmann and Schulte's original manufacturing base established

Triumph's 499cc side-valve engine of 1912 featured the belt drive and exposed valve gear typical of the time.

in 1889, finally closed in 1938. The site later became the operational headquarters of the Gloria Cycle Company, an associated business belonging to Triumph, and it was later used as a sidecar body shop and motorcycle service area. The property was demolished in 1970, but not before serving as Coventry City police force's motorcycle service department.

Car Production

The Triumph Cycle Company moved into car production in 1923 with the 1393cc Triumph Super Seven. Intended to rival the Austin Seven,

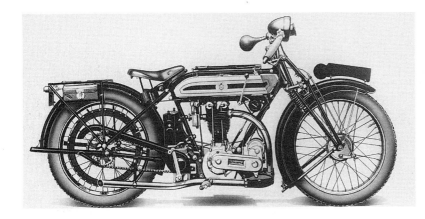

The 1924, 499cc four valves per cylinder 'Ricardo' Triumph roadster, smooth and powerful thanks to its radical multi-valve cylinder head. Designed by Sir Henry Ricardo each pair of valves was set at 90 degrees to each other in an efficient, almost hemispherical combustion chamber. The engine produced 20hp, a commendable figure for an 500cc engine of that period.

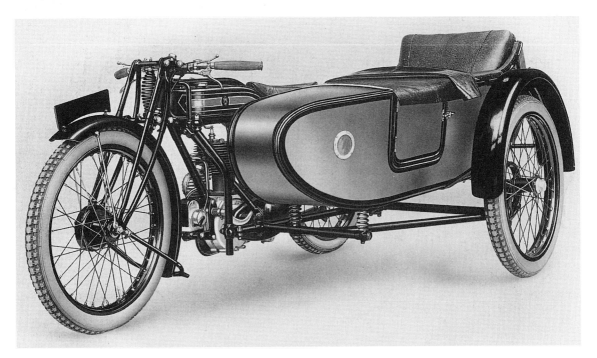

1928 Triumph 494cc Model NP with type L touring sidecar.

the modest and practical Super Seven could reach 47mph (76km/h) and return 35mpg. Competitively priced at less than £200, Triumph's first car met a recognized need and achieved a significant element of success.

In 1934 the company's name was changed to the Triumph Company Limited and in the fol-

lowing year management attention shifted fundamentally. It was decided that the production of 'bread and butter' two wheelers would cease, and in future the company's resources would instead be focused solely on motorcar manufacture. Given the austere nature of the times, Triumph took a decidedly unhealthy interest in

Famous record-breaking rider and engine tuner Victor Horsman with his single-cylinder ohv Triumph racer. Horsman, pictured here at Brooklands where he had an engine tuning shop, developed the 498cc two-valve Model TT sportster engine which superseded the four-valve Ricardo. He provided Triumph with a string of good news stories in the 1920s as he broke successive records on the Brooklands track. Ultimately, in October of 1927 he had pushed the classic hour 500cc speed record to 90.79mph (146.08km/h). After his track career ended, Horsman established a successful motor cycle dealership in Liverpool.

the luxury end of the car market and negotiated production rights to an eight-cylinder 2.3 litre Alfa Romeo.

Triumph resolved to go into production with the eight-cylinder 2300cc Gloria Dolomite, a version of Alfa Romeo's legendary 8C which had won the Le Mans 24-hour endurance race in 1931. The Gloria Dolomite was to be constructed by Triumph under a reciprocal licensing agreement which allowed Alfa to produce and market Triumph's 6/1 650cc vertical-twin motorcycle engine in Italy. In fact Alfa did not take up the manufacturing rights to the 650cc twin-cylinder engine, but just the same the venture into luxury motor manufacturing was to cost Triumph dear.

In spite of the economic depression, and against all the demands of common sense, Triumph pressed ahead with the Gloria Dolomite project. Three cars were assembled in the tool

The 6/1 parallel twin, announced in 1933. Its 650cc engine was strong and reliable but the bike was heavy. The hand change gear shift was seen as old fashioned against the positive stop foot-operated gear change mechanisms that were then becoming the norm.

room of the Priory Street factory in Coventry. As critics had predicted, customers proved hard to find. Soon Lloyds Bank, the company's principal banker, moved to protect its financial interest in the company. Siegfried Bettmann, Triumph's founder and long-standing managing director, was forced to stand down in favour of a Lloyds nominee, Mr Graham, whose main priority would be to manage the company in the best interest of the bank and other creditors.

The company's commercial performance did not improve and in 1935 the Triumph Company Ltd decided to cease motorcycle production completely, sell off the Priory Street factory and focus its dwindling resources on car production at a new plant in Foleshill Road, Holbrooks, Coventry.

Bicycle Manufacture

Associated Cycles, formerly Coventry Bicycles, took over Triumph's pedal cycle business in 1932.

Eventually the bicycle manufacturing business would pass to Raleigh cycles of Nottingham.

Seizing the Opportunity

J.Y. Sangster

At the Ariel motorcycle factory in Selly Oak, Birmingham, news of Triumph's forced decision to sell the Priory Street site came to the attention of John Young Sangster. Just a few years previously, he had staked all he had to finance the purchase of Ariel's premises and equipment after the motorcycle manufacturer had gone into liquidation.

Born in 1896, Sangster had seen army service during the Great War. After returning home he completed the design of a two-cylinder passenger car which the Rover car company had produced and marketed as the Rover 8. Sangster successfully organized factory development and production of the model, but in 1922 he left Rover to become assistant managing director at Components Ltd where his father, Charles Sangster, was already installed as chairman.

Ariel Rescue

Like the rest of British industry, Ariel Motors ran into difficulties in 1929. The struggle lasted until 1932, when the firm was forced into liquidation along with its parent company, Components Ltd

John Young Sangster, often known as 'Jack Sangster' amongst his peers or as 'J.S.' or 'Mr Jack' in the factory, knew that skilled labour laid off by the old Ariel factory was still available locally and that, given the economic conditions of the day, most of the idle staff would be keen to be re-employed. Disregarding the possible conflict of interest posed by his position at Components Ltd, Sangster was able to carefully select key workers and resume Ariel production with a leaner, more competitive company. Equipment was bought from the receiver at rock bottom prices and re-sited in a nearby wheel-rim factory which had been secured by Sangster prior to the old Ariel company's collapse. With only minimal interruption to output the new company, Ariel Motors (JS) Ltd, restarted manufacture of its Red Hunter single-cylinder machine in premises just 500 yards from Ariel's previous address.

The company was restored to commercial viability and went on to prosper. Ariel's success would form the foundation of the modern motorcycle industry in Britain. It is no exaggeration to say that the successful restoration of Ariel was brought about mainly thanks to the work of John Young Sangster, his careful retention of talented staff and the resultant pooling of diverse talents.

In 1928 Edward Turner joined the Ariel design office staff where he produced and developed the brilliantly engineered Ariel Square Four. The rare combination of Sangster's enterprise and Turner's engineering and managerial skills would feature prominently in Triumph's recovery.

Overtures to Triumph

As the winter of 1935 approached, Triumph's unwanted motorcycle operation aroused Sangster's interest.

Aware that news of discussions with any Triumph Company representative would be commercially sensitive and certain to affect the company's valuation, Sangster made discrete initial contact to inquire about a possible deal. His enquiries were met with a positive response and he found that a confidential meeting was possible. In the cloistered privacy of a shared, two-hour train journey from Birmingham to London, Sangster and the Triumph MD, Graham, came to an agreement over the sale of the Triumph Engineering Co. Ltd, which at that time was a non-trading shell company and a dormant subsidiary of Triumph Company Ltd.

Under the agreement, after securing finance for his new firm Sangster would be allowed a short lease on the Priory Street factory with its existing motorcycle production plant and equipment. This arrangement left the two firms, Sangster's Triumph Engineering Company Ltd (motorcycles) and Graham's Triumph Co. Ltd (cars), free to go their separate ways. A further clause gave Sangster an option on the future outright purchase of the Priory Street factory premises and equipment.

Triumph's 1934 6/1 650cc twin. Designed by Val Page, this robust engine featured a gear-driven camshaft and Lucas Magdyno. The four-speed gear box bolted directly onto the back of the crankcase and the primary drive was by helical gears.

These options were exercised soon after the company's successful launch.

The agreement was finalized on 22 January 1936.

Keen to emphasize the continuity of the Triumph name, Sangster invited the founder of the original Triumph Company, Siegfried Bettmann, to take the role of chairman. The invitation was gladly accepted by Bettmann who, although well into his seventies, was still recognized by the workforce, suppliers and dealers as a strong link with the firm's earlier prosperity and the fondly remembered times of greater commercial stability.

The Triumph Engineering Company Ltd

Revitalization of Triumph's motorcycle operation provided Sangster with the opportunity to give Edward Turner greater responsibility. In the

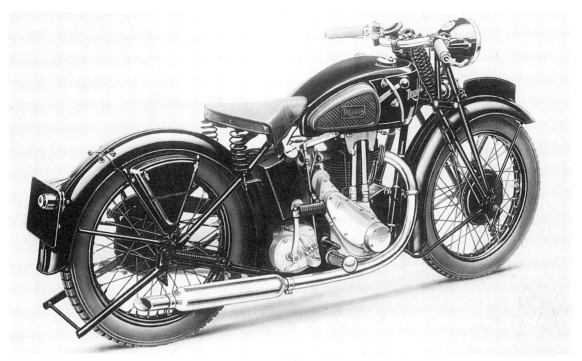

The 1935 493cc 5/2 ohv single with twin exhaust ports, four-speed gearbox and Magdyno lighting. Although this example is equipped with a tank-mounted hand change, a foot-controlled gear lever was available for an extra £1.

The pre-war Tiger 90, part of the Triumph range for 1936. Updated by Edward Turner from Val Page's earlier 500cc 5/5. The 250cc Tiger 70 and 350cc Tiger 80 completed the line up for this first year.

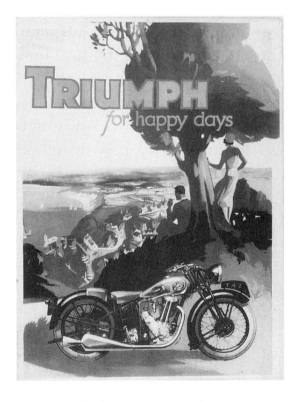

Straight laced and formal in 1914, Triumph's printed material took on a more commercial style as the years progressed.

company hierarchy, the dual roles of Managing Director and Chief Designer were allocated to Turner.

In his managerial guise Turner soon identified possible savings in the sales office. Triumph Sales Manager Harry Perrey was given the freedom of the road along with two other salesmen. Instead of operating from head office they would in future work away from base, each covering triangular segments of the country centred on Triumph's Coventry headquarters. Jack Welton, Perrey's assistant, remained at the Priory Street sales office to process and co-ordinate the anticipated flood of orders.

Quickly settling into his new position as Chief Designer, Turner set to work updating Triumph's model range. Rapid results were needed to provide the fledgling company with the financial reserves that were required in order to develop the entirely new series of bikes that would be crucial to the firm's long-term survival. Turner knew that immediate sales were essential. The result of his efforts was a fleet of attractive single-cylinder machines developed from the old Triumph Company's 2/1 and 3/2 bikes of 1935 and the 1936 5/5. The updated models, renamed Tigers 70, 80 and 90, ranged from 250 to 500cc and, with showroom appeal improved by Turner's imaginative use of chromium plate and silver finishes, they sold well.

2   The Speed Twin

The New Design

The single-cylinder Tigers were only the start. Already Turner was working on a new model destined to alter motorcycle design on a global scale; the 498cc ohv 5T Speed Twin. This 360 degree parallel vertical twin was to set the standard for the British motorcycle industry for years to come. With cylinder dimensions 63 × 80mm and a three-piece crank consisting of two half-cranks bolted to a central flywheel, Turner's new twin was light and compact. This allowed it to be installed in the Tiger 90 frame and to drive through the same gearbox, keeping production changes in the workshop to an absolute minimum. Thanks to these minimal retooling

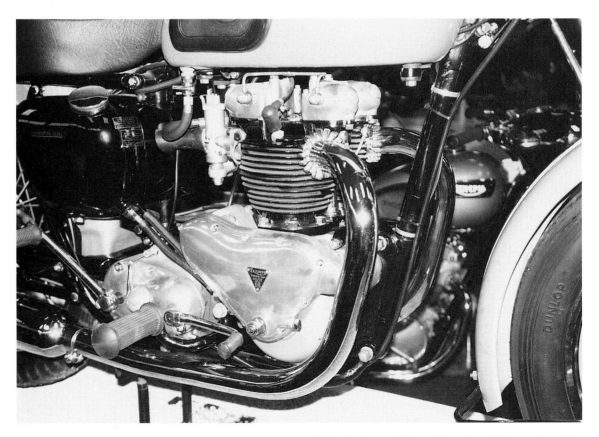

Turner's new twin cylinder 500cc engine was compact enough to be installed in the Tiger 90 frame and drive through the same Tiger 90 gearbox.

Catalogue illustration of the 1938 500cc Speed Twin.

costs, Triumph were able to release the Speed Twin in late July of 1937 priced £75, only £5 more than the single-cylinder Tiger 90. As an added benefit the new twin-cylinder model weighed in at 5lb (2.2kg) less than the single-cylinder version.

To the conservative eye of the customer, the new Speed Twin bore a reassuring resemblance to the single-cylinder Tiger 90, but the similarity ended there; performance was way ahead of the old bike. Riders used to the slow, monotonous thump of the old single were now offered an engine that revved freely to 7,000rpm, reliably delivering usable power right through the range.

Instead of fighting off enraged creditors, two years after its rebirth Triumph Engineering was fighting to meet the demands of keen customers.

The following year, Turner capitalized on his success with the development of a sportier version of the Speed Twin, the Tiger 100. Introduced in 1939 the new model produced 8bhp more than the 5T Speed Twin and was, according to the factory figures, able to reach the 'magic' sales-inducing speed of 100mph. Previous practice had been to list the Tiger models as 70, 80 and 90. This coding indicated the machines best top speed on a good day; in fact it had to be a very good day indeed as the codings were consistently optimistic. The Tiger's extra power was achieved by increasing the compression ratio, polishing the engine internals to reduce oil drag and fitting a larger carburettor to improve induction. For the weekend clubman racer, megaphone silencers with detachable ends were also fitted. Compared to similar products of the day the Tiger 100 was light and easily managed. Power was delivered smoothly and the motor was responsive, almost twitchy in its eagerness to be off. Keenly priced at just £80, demand for the sporty Tiger 100 soon overtook even the Speed Twin.

War . . .

Celebration of the Tiger 100's success was overtaken by the outbreak of World War II. In response to the new threat Triumph promptly set to work manufacturing despatch motorcycles,

A Tiger 100 in full sporting trim and fitted with a sprung hub rear wheel, the rider is Percy Tait.

generator sets and other equipment for military use. Triumph's new twin-cylinder engines were not seen as ideal for service life and so the 3HW, a 350cc ohv single-cylinder machine developed from the pre-war 3H, became Triumph's standard military mount.

In November 1940 the centre of Coventry suffered a series of severe air raids and the Triumph factory at Priory Street, home to Triumph since 1907, was forced to cease production. Manufacturing resumed at The Cape (later nicknamed the Cape of Good Hope), a temporary canal-side factory site in Warwick. By mid-1942, with government assistance, the company was able to move to a permanent purpose-built factory outside Coventry near the village of Meriden. The new address, Meriden Road, Allesley, would be home for the company for the next four decades. It was here that Triumph, as part of its contribution to military research, produced two prototypes of a small lightly armoured track-laying vehicle. Powered by a 50cc two-stroke engine, this machine was designed to carry a lone soldier and his rifle into battle. However, this single-seater fighting vehicle was not a success.

. . . and Peace!

The end of hostilities in 1945 left Triumph in a difficult position. On the one hand, it had a range of proven and popular twin-cylinder machines ready for immediate manufacture and a modern factory to make them in; but, on the other hand, the company faced a severe shortage of the raw materials with which to make them.

The would-be customer faced a shortage of his own: in other words, the money to pay for bikes or, indeed, any other consumer durable. With war work overtime finished, the man on the street found that money was tight. Manufacturers came to recognize that post-war austerity had made a commercial minefield of the marketplace.

Shrewdly, Turner adopted a siege-style economy that would nurse the company through the tricky financial period ahead. On 1 March 1945 Triumph's post war product line-up was announced. The model range comprized the twin-cylinder 500cc Speed Twin and Tiger 100 plus the ohv 343cc girder-forked 3H, which was essentially the military 3HW smartened up with

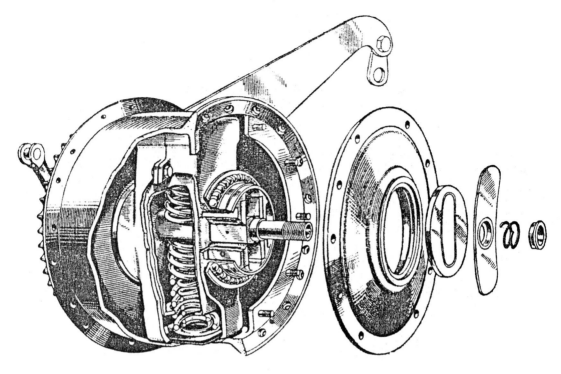

The unique Triumph Spring Wheel hub first appeared on Ernie Lyons' 500cc for his 1946 Senior Manx Grand Prix win. It was later made available on roadgoing 5Ts and T100s.

black-and-white lining. Polished engine castings and a chromium-plated exhaust pipe further improved the old war-horse but could not completely disguise its dated origins. As soon as the wartime stockpiles of 3HW parts were exhausted the civilianized 3H was quietly dropped from the product range.

To make best use of the limited materials available, only the top sellers of the range, the twins (now equipped with an innovative telescopic front fork) continued as Triumph's post-war products. Cold-hearted finance dictated that for the next two years only the 500cc Speed Twin and Tiger 100 would carry the Triumph logo.

The Tiger 100 offered in 1945 was not quite the bike that it had been pre-war. No longer was each machine supplied with its own, individual, dynamometer test certificate. Possibly due to the reduced octane rating of post-war petrol, power had dropped from a claimed 34bhp at 7,000rpm to 30bhp at 6,500rpm.

By 1947 the two 500s had been joined by the 350cc 3T. Also offered for the first time in 1947 was Turner's infamous sprung-hub rear suspension option. Although of limited benefit to the rider, the dubious merits of the sprung hub, available in either MkI/MkII or mark two form, did at least allow Triumph to delay the expense of developing a new frame with proper rear suspension.

All-Alloy Engine

In 1948 the off-road Trophy TR5 and competition Grand Prix were introduced. The Grand Prix, priced at £342 18s 0d, featured an all-alloy engine that made effective use of castings previously intended only for war service. Ernie Lyons, Irish farmer and successful road racer, had used the alloy head and cylinder to seize victory in September 1946 when he competed in the first post-war Senior Manx Grand Prix. The all-alloy

The Tiger 100A. This was the first sporting version of the unit construction 5TA Speed Twin.

engine that powered him to victory had been developed by Freddie Clark, Triumph's Experimental Department Chief. Two years later Triumph made the same combination of parts available to the public as part of its range of competition machines for 1948.

The 'square barrel' finning on the GPs and Trophys carried tell-tale lugs showing them to be wartime production castings originally designed for the Air Ministry. These lugs had originally carried air ducting for the cooling system of the static-mounted power-plant engine. The 1946 500cc alloy race winner had been developed from components intended for the engine that drove the lightweight airborne generator sets (officially known as Airborne Auxiliary Power Plants or AAPP) used to power radar installations in Lancaster and Halifax bombers.

1950

1950 marked the start of the 'Second Golden Age of Motorcycling'. The industry's UK sales graph started to lift off as Britain became the largest manufacturer of motorcycles in the world. During 1950, over 700,000 motorcycles would be registered for home use.

In the search for a larger slice of the growing world market for motorcycles, the immediate priority for Triumph became more power. 'Performance, Stamina, and Quality' were the priorities listed in the 1950 sales brochure. As a businessman, Turner recognized that the North American market offered a rare and possibly unique opportunity for post-war commercial growth. He also knew that to exploit the US market Triumph would have to increase the size

The origins of Ernie Lyons's Senior Manx Grand Prix winning engine of 1946 lay in the power unit that drove these generator sets. Officially known as Airborne Auxiliary Power Plants or AAPPs, the sets were used to power the radar installations carried in Lancaster and Halifax bombers.

A Triumph 498cc Grand Prix, featuring the silicon-alloy head and cylinder barrel originally intended for the generator set, competing at Brough Airfield in 1954.

of its 500cc twin. Continued development of the engine in search of increased power would soon start to compromise reliability. The displacement of a typical home market American motorcycle of the day was 45cu.in. (750cc) and to compete, in both sporting and commercial terms, Triumph's 500cc twin would have to be upped to 650cc, the maximum displacement Turner felt appropriate for his twin-cylinder engine.

As anticipated, increasing the bore to 71mm and the stroke to 82mm brought significant improvements in mid-range torque and top speed, both crucial characteristics for the US market. The bike would be required to reach 100mph (160km/h) and be able to maintain high cruising speeds for as long as the rider required. Whether covering the distance in high-speed touring or in the heat of competition, the message was clear: for the US market, size clearly mattered.

The 500cc Grand Prix engine showing the silicon alloy cylinder head and barrel, which originated from the lightweight generator set, mounted on the Tiger 100 crankcase.

Edward Turner, pictured here in November 1951. Turner started work at Ariel in 1929 and by 1930 had designed the Square Four, a machine which remained in production until 1952. After taking over from Val Page as Chief Designer at Ariel in 1932 Turner made the move to Triumph in 1936 where he became Chief Designer and General Manager when J.Y. Sangster took over motorcycle production.

Triumph's Monthlhery endurance event featured prominently at the Earls Court show of 1949. As intended, the resulting international publicity placed Triumph's new top of the range 650cc Thunderbird firmly in the limelight.

Symptomatic of later problems, static design policy was being eulogized as a positive feature even in 1951.

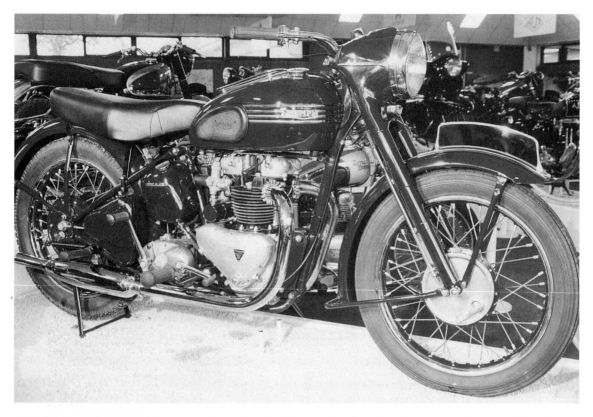

1950 5T Speed Twin. In 1949 instruments and controls previously mounted on the tank-top instrument panel were re-sited on the newly introduced headlamp nacelle. The following year the chromium plated petrol tank was discontinued on all models apart from the TR5 Trophy.

Thunderbird and the Montlhery Endurance Event

The new model, the 649cc 6T Thunderbird, lived up to the requirement in every way. To prove it, Triumph organized a typical public relations event to demonstrate the company's faith in the new bike. Established designer and astute business man Turner now turned showman by despatching three brand new Thunderbirds, a team of five riders and full support crew to the racing circuit at Montlhery Autodrome, outside Paris. Detailed arrangements for the event were made by Tyrell Smith and Ernie Nott, both successful pre-war racers. The five riders were Alex Scobie, Len Bayliss, Bob Manns, Allan Jefferies and Jimmy Alves. Official ACU observer at the venue was

Harold Taylor, later to be Britain's moto-cross team manager.

Three 'fresh from the factory' production bikes were ridden to the track and, on 20 September 1949, hurled around the banked circuit for 500 miles. Although speeds averaged 90mph (145km/h), thanks to the Thunderbird's low 7 to 1 compression ratio the local 72-octane fuel presented no problem. The event progressed smoothly until Len Bayliss, on machine number 3, was forced to make a stop with a split petrol tank. Later, whilst being ridden by Allan Jeffries, the same bike gave trouble when the chain guard came loose and had to be removed. For the final lap the bikes were ridden side by side at 100mph (160km/h). The fastest lap of the day was covered

Drive-side engine detail of the 1959 T110.

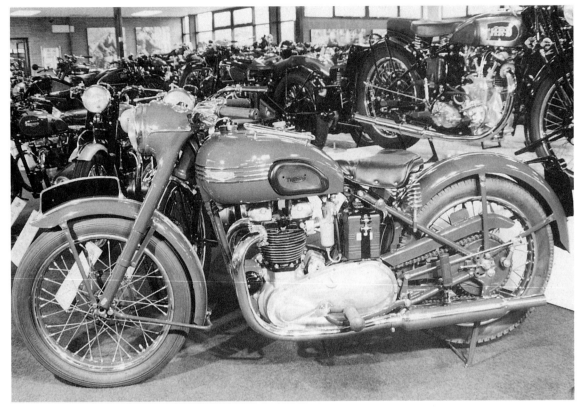

1950 650cc Thunderbird. The addition of an extra 150cc produced a startling improvement in performance.

by Bob Manns at 101.78mph (163.76km/h). Under the admiring gaze of the world's motoring press the bikes were then triumphantly ridden home.

In today's jaded world, such promotions might be seen as mere hype, but in 1949 credit was given for style and originality. Even the sceptical Parisienne Police were sufficiently impressed to place an order for their first consignment of Thunderbirds and repeat orders followed. The model subsequently became standard issue for traffic patrol duties in Paris and many other cities. Later, the 6TP (the 650cc Saint) would be specifically developed and marketed internationally for police patrol work.

Inevitably, Triumph's Thunderbird endurance event at the Montlhery circuit featured prominently in the Earl's Court show of that year and, as intended, the international publicity generated placed Triumph's new top of the range 650 firmly in the limelight.

Tiger T110

The 650cc T-bird immediately won the hearts of enthusiasts at home and in the US. Privateer racers and tuning shops tried the same 'go faster' techniques that they had already applied to the robust 500cc engine and, predictably, they worked. The 649cc engine's US competition success in events such as the Catalina and Big Bear Run were not ignored by the factory and, true to form, in 1953

Many of the modifications applied and thoroughly tested on the American race tracks were present in the Tiger 110; plus, for the first time on any Triumph, the all new 'High Movement' swinging arm rear suspension. A well-overdue improvement on the sprung hub.

The high performance version of the Thunderbird, the 1954 T110 featured bigger valves, high compression pistons and, for the first time on any Triumph, swinging arm rear suspension.

the Tiger 110, the sports version of the Thunderbird, was announced.

The modifications applied and so thoroughly tested on the American race tracks were present in the Tiger 110. In addition, the Tiger 110 sported the all-new swinging arm rear suspension, a larger carburettor and the high-lift E3325 camshaft (previously known as the 'Q' sports camshaft Q1481/2 and made available exclusively to those with special influence gained through competition success). These, together with high compression pistons and bigger valves, all contributed to the T110's extra urge. To slow the machine from its official 110mph (177km/h) top speed (at the time 117mph (188km/h) was claimed by an enthusiastic motorcycling press) a larger 8in front brake was fitted.

Triumph sold to BSA

On 15 March 1951 as the 650cc Thunderbird was being developed into the T110, Triumph was taken over by BSA (Birmingham Small Arms). When BSA had bought Ariel from Jack Sangster in 1944, it had been agreed that if Triumph were ever to be sold, Sangster would ensure that first refusal was offered to BSA. That sale was now imminent. Fear that punitive death duties would compromise Triumph's commercial integrity dictated that Sangster rationalize his personal financial position. A prime step in that process was disposal of the company. The asking price was £2,448,000 and BSA was more than happy to pay. Sangster received 90 per cent of the proceeds with 10 per cent going to Turner, in line with their respective holdings in the company at the time.

Throughout these unsettling developments

1959 T110 Tiger 110, restored to factory-fresh condition.

Motoring conditions were different in 1951, but it is difficult to believe that they were ever this good: just the same the message is clear, 'on a Triumph you can leave your troubles, and the rest of the traffic, far behind'.

'Triumph the best Motorcycle in the World'. This is one caption that I, for one, will not argue with; although others might.

1955 Speed Twin, now equipped with swinging arm rear suspension.

Turner's grip on Triumph company policy remained firm. The Meriden plant continued to trade successfully at home and abroad. BSA, the new parent company headquartered at Small Heath, allowed Triumph's Meriden factory to continue with established policies and working practice throughout the fifties. A keenly fought rivalry in the various branches of motorcycle sport and marketing existed, but commercial co-operation between Triumph's Meriden and BSA's Small Heath factories was maintained.

In 1956, the BSA Automotive Division was formed with Edward Turner as Chief Executive. This was made up of the Ariel, BSA and Triumph motorcycle companies, the car, bus and specialist vehicle manufacturer Daimler, and Carbodies of Coventry, builder of the familiar London taxicab. Turner divided the bulk of his time between Triumph and turning round the fortunes of the unprofitable Daimler operation. Production costs at Daimler were rapidly reduced and the model range radically revized around two Turner designed V8 engines, one with $2\frac{1}{2}$ litre and the other with $4\frac{1}{2}$ litre capacity. The $2\frac{1}{2}$ litre unit was used in the Daimler SP250 sports car and later, after Daimler was sold to Jaguar in 1960, in the Mark II Jaguar body shell to be marketed as the Daimler V8.

3 Triumph Corporation of America

Recognizing the Potential Market

The Triumph Corporation of America was established in 1951 to supply the Midwest and Eastern States. Wholly owned by the Meriden factory, the organization was founded in response to the idea that untapped demand for Triumph machines existed in the United States.

West Coast retailer Johnson Motors Inc. of Pasadena, California had shown that the potential motorcycle market was good in California, but even greater sales potential was felt to exist elsewhere in the United States. Turner suspected that the American Midwest, Southern States and the US Atlantic seaboard would all provide similar rewards.

To prove it, Turner again drew on personal contacts, this time in the field of marketing. Percival White, president of the Market Research Corporation of America, was a friend of Turner's and a fellow two-wheeler enthusiast. White was a keen collector of motorcycles and especially interested in Douglas machines. This personal interest in the industry and his professional expertise made him ideally qualified to carry out the market study which Turner required.

In charge of European accounts at White's Market Research Corporation was a man who had direct links with the heartland of British engineering. Born in Coventry in 1901, Denis McCormack had been engaged by the Beardmore Precision engineering company in King's Norton, Birmingham. From there he had moved to Wolsley Motors before crossing the Atlantic and finding work in the field of market research. An early project for McCormack was to research the marketing problems that would finally finish off the venerable Indian Motorcycle Company.

McCormack and the Market Research Corporation were able to confirm Turner's intuition that potential for Triumph in the Midwest and East Coast America looked every bit as good as in California. To exploit that potential to the full, Turner established the US-based Triumph Corporation of America (Tricor). Based in Maryland, Ohio and set up as a wholly-owned subsidiary of the Meriden parent company, Tricor took care of distribution for the Eastern US market from 1951 onwards.

Not everybody involved was completely happy. Predictably, Bill Johnson of Johnson Motors Inc. had hoped to secure distribution rights for the whole of the United States. Correspondence from Edward Turners' office shows that Johnson's hope had initially been encouraged. Factory policy had changed when Turner realized that an element of in-house competition might introduce added zest, and increased sales, to the business.

McCormack's research proved accurate and thorough. Keenly aware of the US motorcycle market's true potential, and consequently ideally qualified for the top job with the new distribution company, McCormack was appointed president of Tricor at the age of forty-eight. As a consolation for his disappointment in not securing a wider market for his own operation, Bill Johnson was made Vice President.

Harley Davidson, looking forward to a monopoly position in its home market after the demise of Indian motorcycles, was enraged to find a foreign manufacturer moving in on its territory. Using tactics that might nowadays be

The showrooms of West Coast motorcycle retailer Johnson Motors Inc. at 267 West Colorado Street, Pasadena.

considered decidedly anti-competitive, Harley pressurized its existing dealers into refusing additional franchises from Tricor. Instead new dealers, many of them ex-servicemen starting out in business for the first time, had to be appointed and trained by Tricor and Johnson Motors. In the face of the opposition of established American motorcycle industry McCormack mapped out a new dealer network and made a success of the Triumph Corporation.

Once established, Tricor achieved remarkable success. In 1965 nearly 9,000 machines were sold through its retailers. With Johnson Motors Inc operating from Pasedena to supply West Coast dealers and Tricor serving the Eastern territory from its Baltimore HQ, total exports of Triumph motorcycles to the US rose to 15,338 in 1965; 6,531 via Johnson Motors and 8,807 through the Triumph Corporation. On his occasional visits to the Meriden factory in his new role McCormack proved to be a popular figure. No doubt this was largely due to his personality, but the upward slant of Tricor's sales figures could only have added to his well-deserved popularity. Ultimately more Triumph motorcycles would be sold in the United States than in any other country; including Triumph's country of origin, Great Britain.

The designer label that packed a powerful sales punch in America during the 1950s and 1960s.

In 1967 Triumph were presented with the Queen's Award to Industry. That year saw 80 per cent of the company's output going for export, mostly to the United States.

Export T120s destined for the United States receive finishing touches at Meriden in the mid-1960s.

American Desert Racing

From the late 1950s until the early 1970s the not-so-subtle sport of motorcycle desert racing flourished in the western States of the United States.

Broadly similar to European enduro events, albeit staged on a much grander scale, desert racing was made possible thanks to the vast empty spaces available in expansive venues such as California's Mojave Desert and Mexico's Baja peninsula. In these remote and deserted locations, competitors could indulge in mass starts and high-speed pursuits across varied and challenging terrain. For the riders danger existed in the shape of hidden ravines, unexpected rough ground and clumps of spiky cactus. Unexpected contact with local wildlife, such as the occasional yucca tree anchored to the desert floor by a tenacious root system, could all too quickly reverse the normal ecological roles, suddenly placing man and machine on the endangered species list.

Baja 1000

The Baja (pronounced Bah-ha) 1000 was first staged in 1966. Organised entirely by, and intended primarily for, American riders, the Baja 1000 covered the length of the Baja peninsula. Running between what was then a shabby shanty-town border crossing at Tijuana and the southern city of La Paz, the event was run as a straight 1,000 mile point-to-point race. Popular motorbikes entered in the original competitions of the early seventies included Swedish 360 and 450cc Husqvarnas and Italian-built two-stroke Harley-Davidsons from the Aermacchi factory. Although the occasional Britbike competed, the vast majority of two-wheeled Baja entrants rode Japanese machines. By 1975, Harley-Davidson was successfully campaigning a specially prepared version of its SX250 trail bike in the Baja.

Entrants used cross-country routes and the poorly paved roads of the impoverished region as they saw fit. During the early years, ordinary traffic and the local populace remained at risk for the twenty-hour duration of the event, but by the mid-1970s, after proper tarmac highways had been constructed and due regard was paid to ecological and social considerations, Baja organizers were obliged to impose restrictions. The course was shortened to a 1,000km (600 mile) loop starting and finishing at Ensenada, just south of the original Tijuana start point.

Although shorter, the new course was very much more demanding than the early point-to-point route. The course revisions fundamentally changed the character of the event and serious Baja contenders of the late 1970s were more likely to enter four-wheel drive cars and specialist military off-road trucks than motorcycles.

Barstow–Las Vegas Run

Another classic American enduro event was the annual Barstow to Las Vegas race. Hundreds of competitors would nose up to a single start line before hurling their machines through 500 miles of open Californian desert scrubland and across the state line into Nevada, where a fortunate few would finish in Las Vegas.

What had been previously regarded as wasteland became cherished areas of wildlife sanctuary and parkland. As concern for the environment grew, event organizers were forced to limit the number of entrants and restrict the enormous areas previously covered by the events. Instead of an initial rip-roaring charge across the desert, staggered starts were introduced to minimize the destruction of vulnerable plant life.

Inevitably, after research into the damage done to desert vegetation by such large concentrations of motorbikes, the influential Californian environmental lobby prevailed upon the State Government to ban the event.

Big Bear Run

First staged in the early 1920s 'The Big Bear Run' laid justified claim to being 'the world's largest motorized race'. Held in January, 'the Bear' was organized by the Orange County Club on California's Pacific Coast. A typical event would field more than 500 competitors through a rigorous 150 mile route across the Mojave Desert. Along the way mud, snow and sand had to be crossed at speed with occasional respite coming where the trail took to the narrow fire roads that cut through the scrub. These isolated tracks normally gave emergency vehicles access to remote forest fires that sometimes flared in the area. Even in the rare patches of shade temperatures could soar to 110° Fahrenheit.

The demanding conditions favoured the lighter British machines against the home-grown heavy-weight Indians and Harley-Davidsons, but riders of all machines endured severe privations in the chase to the chequered flag. Finishing the course was an achievement, and a place on the winner's rostrum was considered an honour.

Of the 626 riders who set out on the 151 mile course in the 1956 Big Bear Run, just 92 finished within the required schedule. Leader of the pack that year was Bill Postal with a winning time of 4 hours 7 minutes. Second was Bud Ekins and third Arvin Cox; each rode a version of the newly introduced 649cc Triumph TR6 Trophy.

The Bikes

A very special type of machine evolved to meet the challenge presented by these events. Similar to moto-cross competition bikes, US desert racing required a machine with greater stamina and increased reserves of power.

Although Edward Turner was reluctant to commit Triumph's development resources to the UK's domestic racing calendar, he recognized that the US market demanded special consideration. The popularity of US enduro-type desert racing guaranteed increased sales if a production machine which was ready and able to compete successfully could be supplied.

Heavily modified privately entered Triumph machines had continued to score repeated US successes over the years. These competitor-initiated performance-enhancing modifications were carefully monitored by Triumph's American distributors and filtered back to the development workshop at Meriden where they could be perfected and incorporated into mainstream design. Both the Tiger 110 and the Trophy benefited from this source of technical inspiration. When it was introduced in 1956, the 649cc Trophy proved to be an ideal desert race contender and by 1960 the theme had been developed into the TR7B Bonneville Scrambler, a machine equipped for street use but ready for rapid transformation for the track.

The concept was further refined in 1963. Johnson Motors, the US West Coast Triumph distributor, resolved to produce a version of the Bonneville to contest these fiercely competitive desert and dirt track events. Using the frame and many of the standard cycle parts of the T120C, the competition sports model of the T120R street Bonne, Johnson Motors upped the compression ratio to a claimed 12:1, although in truth only 11.2:1 pistons were fitted. Fuel was fed into the combustion chamber through a pair of oversize 13/16 Amal Monobloc carbs and the T120C's street-legal silencers were replaced with straight-through end pipes mounted on the high-level exhaust system. Later versions had large-bore open-ended pipes tucked in tightly under the frame's lower rails and finishing short beneath the swinging arm pivot.

The result, the lean and mean T120C TT Bonneville TT Special, was both visually stunning and competitively

From the late 1950s until the early 1970s the not-so-subtle sport of motorcycle desert racing flourished in the Western States of the United States.

American Desert Racing *continued*

effective. Ridden by Skip Van Leeuwen on its first outing the TT Special led the field home at Southern California's Ascot Park TT, and from there on in the successes just kept on coming. The TT Special's claim to be the fastest standard motorcycle went unchallenged at the time but, lest there be any doubt, the US magazine *Cycle World* achieved 123.5mph (198.7km/h) when testing a 1963 version. By 1965, the T120C Competition Sports Bonneville accounted for more wins in US enduro-type competition than all other makes combined.

During the model's four-year production life span the TT was successfully put to work in enduros, drag racing heats and TT scrambles. With minimal modification the TT Special could be registered for US road use and, given the bike's high sporting profile, it soon became the transport of choice for many young, and not so young, dudes seeking enhanced street cred.

Although plans had been made to continue the model into 1968, production was discontinued in 1967 after approximately 3,500 TT Specials had been manufactured.

More machines leave the factory for export to the United States. Despite 60 per cent of Meriden production being allocated for US export, the demands of the American market could not be supplied fast enough.

4 Breaking Records

Record Attempt on the Salt Flats

In 1955 Johnny Allen, a 26-year-old from Fort Worth, Texas, drove his Thunderbird powered streamliner at 193.72mph (311.70km/h) each way over the flying start mile at Bonneville Salt Flats, near Wendover, Utah. The engine which powered Allen's 14ft long cigar-shaped two-wheeler was a 649cc Triumph twin running with a cast iron cylinder head and barrel. Essentially, this was a standard Thunderbird top end driving a forged billet, one-piece crankshaft with plain bearing Cadillac big end shells. Allen's engine had been built by Jack Wilson, a Triumph motorcycle dealer and noted engine tuner from Dallas. The aerodynamic bodyshell and the record-breaking bike beneath, a new concept in world record attempts, had been designed by pilot 'Stormy' Mangham during his time off work at American Airlines. The whole venture was sponsored by Johnson Motors of Pasadena.

The following year Allen's achievement was topped by a German NSU team. They upped the record to 211.4mph (340.1km/h) using a super-charged 498cc dohc twin, a modified version of the machine which had pushed the record to 180.17mph (289.89 km/h) in 1951, when the bid had been made on home ground using a closed-off section of the Munich to Ingolstadt autobahn. Within days after the dust had settled on their Bonneville success and the Germans had left for home, Allen fired up his cigar-shaped machine for another attempt.

On 6 September 1956 he skimmed across the salt to an absolute motorcycle world speed record. Running on a nitro-methane fuel, the two-wheeled missile clocked 214.4mph (345km/h) each way along the Bonneville Salt Flats. Confident of success, Allen and his team packed up and left the Flats to the wildlife.

In April 1957, following months of argument over the official accreditation of the time-keeper, the Federation Internationale Motcycliste (FIM), controlling body for such record attempts, rejected Allen's claim to the record. In America the FIM's objections were ignored. Even in Europe the protracted controversy served only to heighten public awareness of Triumph's contribution to what was generally seen as a successful record-breaking achievement. Turner capitalized on the quarrel by commissioning a transfer depicting a speedbird with the uncompromising slogan 'The World's Fastest Motorcycle'.

More Power

Officially acknowledged or not, Allen's 214mph run was seen as a tremendous success for Triumph. As news of the disputed speed record spread, demand for even more performance from Triumph's production bikes increased. Typically, Turner would not be pressured into any premature policy decisions on performance improvements. Neither would he make any further factory commitment to racing. Customers with enquiries regarding increased output from Triumph's machines continued to be referred to the high performance tuning parts list, a list which, notwithstanding the factory's reluctance, slowly grew in size. Customers were, of course, warned that any unauthorized modification would invalidate the terms of the manufacturer's guarantee.

Now at rest at the National Motorcycle Museum in Birmingham, Johnny Allen's streamliner once crossed the Bonneville Salt Flats in Utah at 214mph (344km/h) and became the centre of an international controversy.

Triumph-powered world-record beater: Johnny Allen and team at Bonneville Salt Flats, Utah USA. Team members are (left to right) Jack Wilson (mechanic); 'Stormy' Maugham (airflow designer); Wilbur Cedar (Secretary of Johnson Motors); Bill Johnson (President of Johnson Motors); John Bough (Lucas rep); Johnny Allen (driver). On 5 October 1955 Allen achieved 192mph (309km/h) over the measured mile. On 6 September the following year he upped the record to 193mph (311km/h).

Johnny Allen's unsupercharged 214mph World Motorcycle Speed Record contender.

Despite this reluctance, in 1956 a concession towards increased performance from production machines was made. The T110 and the new TR6 Trophy 650cc were fitted with a new alloy cylinder head. Known as the 'Delta' head due to its shape, the new casting allowed the fitting of dual carburettors. It was introduced to cope with the hotter engine operating temperatures that resulted from burning the newly available increased octane fuels at higher, more efficient, compression ratios. The following year Meriden produced a consignment of Tiger100/RS racing machines for export to the United States. The bikes were equipped with twin carbs mounted on cylinder heads re-engineered from the 650cc Delta head casting.

The twin-carburettor Delta head for the 500cc motor was in fact already listed as a tuning aid in the Triumph Corporation of America's catalogue. The appearance of the head, complete with twin carbs, on factory-prepared 500cc machines produced a frenzy of demand for the same installation to be made on the 650cc engine. The die for the new cylinder head casting had been produced in 1955 in anticipation of the introduction of the single-carburettor 650cc T110 and TR6. In addition to coping with the increased combustion temperatures produced by the higher than normal compression ratios, the new alloy head featured internal oil drains which discharged through the push rod tubes, allowing the previous external oil drains to be deleted.

Unfortunately, early examples of the Delta head suffered cracking between the cylinder head bolts and valve seats. Consequently a reshaped combustion chamber with smaller valve apertures was introduced on the casting for 1958. New pistons with a remodelled crown profile and smaller valve cut-outs were also introduced. Although reliability improved, the performance of the original pattern castings was never matched.

Later in 1958, a 650cc a twin carburettor die-cast alloy cylinder head with splayed inlet ports was included in the 'replacement parts' catalogue. Now, with all of the major components listed and available through official channels, it could only be a matter of time before the Bonneville was born.

5　The Birth of the Bonnie

Prototyping

Triumph Engineering's Experimental Instruction Sheet 419 could almost be considered to be the birth certificate of the Triumph Bonneville. Dated 19 March 1958, the sheet details a 650cc T110 engine equipped with splayed port cylinder head, twin type 6 carburettors, E3134 inlet camshaft and 8.5 to 1 compression ratio pistons. Tabled on the sheet are the results of the day's testing and the condition of the engine after those tests. After having produced 48.8bhp on the factory's dynamometer the engine had been stripped, examined, and found to have no faults. The remarks column of Sheet 419 noted that 'Mr Turner expressed satisfaction' with the results and the condition of the engine. Entries made under the heading 'Further Instructions' authorized

1959 649cc T120 Bonneville. During its first year of production the model followed the house style of the Thunderbird and carried the same touring equipment.

Frank Baker, then head of Triumph's experimental department, to rebuild the engine and fit it into a T110 frame ready for high-speed track testing at MIRA, the Motor Industries Research Association establishment at Lindley, near Nuneaton.

Like Johnny Allen at Bonneville, Triumph had recognized that the three-piece bolted-up crank used on the original 500cc Speed Twin could not handle the higher power produced by the twin-carburettor 650. Allen's solution, as used in his controversial 1956 214mph Bonneville record run, had been a one-piece forged 'billet' crank running with Cadillac automobile big end bearings. For the embryonic Bonneville, Triumph also used a one-piece forged crank, this time with a bolted-on cast iron flywheel. The flywheel was fitted to the crank by passing it over the timing side end of the shaft and locating it on to a central web of the crankshaft forging. Three radial bolts passed through the outer periphery of the flywheel into threaded holes in the crankshaft mounting web. Even this robust crank/flywheel assembly went through three different design stages before the final version proved acceptable. By 1963 the ultimate crank/flywheel assembly provided an 85 per cent balance factor, a factor that remained the established standard for the life of the 650cc T120, only changing with the introduction of the T140.

Like the bolted-up crankshaft, the six-plate Tiger 110 clutch and the single-leading-shoe front brake were also now operating on the margins of their design capabilities. During trials

Detail shot showing the shared remote float chamber and the 'chopped' Amal monobloc carburettors initially deemed necessary to allow installation of the twin carburettor set-up.

of the prototype twin-carburettor T110 (or the Bonneville to be) Percy Tait, the respected racer and factory test rider, had managed an electronically timed 128mph only to find himself running out of test track as he slowed.

Turner himself still viewed the T120 project with mixed feelings. In a theatrical declaration made in August 1958, as a smart two-tone dark blue and grey prototype Bonneville was revealed to engineering and marketing staff, Turner warned Frank Baker, Triumph's head of product development (and anyone else who might be listening) that '. . . this, my boy, will lead us straight into Carey Street'. At the time Carey Street was the location of the dreaded corporate bankruptcy courts.

However, after further prototype machines were built and tested on public roads and the research centre test track, Turner's doubts were dispelled. In late August 1958 he gave the twin-carb T110 project production clearance. Also agreed at that August meeting in Triumph's experimental workshop was the prototype bike's new name. With memories of Johnny Allen's exploits in Utah still fresh there could be only one choice. Amongst the assembled group, especially the American contingent of dealers and marketeers, 'Big Bill' Johnson of Johnson Motors Inc, Wilbur Ceder and Denis McCormack of the Triumph Corporation of America, the name Triumph 'Bonneville' was greeted with general and enthusiastic acclaim.

1958 Launch

Even though the 1958 Earl's Court Show was rapidly approaching and the new season's sales catalogue had already been produced, it was hastily decided that the new model should be released in time to head Triumph's product range for 1959. The 1959 Retail Price list had been printed in September 1958 and initially listed the Bonneville as a 500cc machine. For launch date the list was quickly corrected by over-printing the entry to show the bike as an ohv twin 650cc, costing £294 8s 3d. Despite the rushed preparation and the lack of sales

brochures, the Bonneville stood out as the star attraction at Earl's Court.

Although to the uneducated eye the Bonneville might have appeared to be no more than a twin-carbed T110, the truth was that the new bike represented an inspired combination of technical development and competitive endeavour. The unbridled, often excessive, enthusiasm of private entrant racing teams had been tempered by more sober judgement in Triumph's experimental department. The production Bonneville represented the pick of many performance-enhancing racing modifications, some good, some not so good, refined into practical and reliable form. Factory production of the 650cc Bonneville, top of Triumph's new 1959 range, started on 4 September 1958.

For that initial year the Bonneville followed much of the Tiger 110's styling. Despite its claimed sports bike heritage the machine featured deeply valanced, touring style mudguards and Triumph's trademark nacelle housing the headlamp, light switch, ammeter and speedometer. The nacelle, styled by Turner's personal assistant and drawing office aide-de-camp Jack Wickes, was introduced in 1949. Although the two-piece streamlined metal cowling tidied up the mess of cables and controls that converge around the headlamp area of any bike, the nacelle had the disadvantage of being unable to accommodate two full-size instruments and, as all enthusiasts know, a sports bike without speedo and tachometer mounted as a matched pair must be regarded as deficient in instrumentation.

In previous years Triumph speedometers had been marked with concentric scales indicating the engine rpm for a given road speed in each of the top three gears. Known briefly as the 'revolator', these were little more than a technical novelty, and dedicated sports riders preferred a proper rev counter. If the bike was to be taken seriously by true enthusiasts, the touring bike 'tin wear' and the nacelle would have to go and proper provision made for the fitting of an optional tachometer.

Customer reaction to the touring bike trim combined with the 'pearl grey', 'tangerine' and

The original Bonneville's nacelle housed the headlamp, light switch, ammeter and speedometer. Although it tidied up the mess of cables and controls that converge around the headlamp of any bike, it was unable to accommodate both a full-size speedometer and a tachometer.

The Bonneville 650 led the Triumph range into the 1959 season and continued to head the field for decades to come.

gold lining colour scheme was mixed. Some felt the garish 'tangerine' jarred with the staid and sombre touring fittings, others felt that the colour was great and it was the heavy tin wear that was out of place. Either way the criticism struck home. Before the year was out, an alternative 'pearl grey' and 'azure blue' combination (actually a tasteful two-tone blue-on-blue colour scheme) was offered. The following year the nacelle was dropped.

6 Early Bonnevilles

T120 Bonneville 1959

1959 649cc T120 Bonneville

The first Bonneville of the series shared the heavy mudguards and nacelle common to the rest of the Triumph 650 range. The twin carburettor pre-unit construction engine and gearbox were carried in the same black-painted single downtube frame used by the T110. The battery box and oil tank were also painted black and the two-level twinseat was covered in black vinyl with white piping. The mudguards were finished in 'pearl grey' with a 'tangerine' centre stripe lined in gold and the petrol tank sported a 'pearl grey' top half with a 'tangerine' lower section separated by gold lining.

Price: £294 8s 3d
Commencing engine number 020076

Engine

Cylinder bore	71mm
Stroke	82 mm
Cylinder capacity	649cc (40cu.in)
Compression ratio	8.5:1
Claimed output	46bhp at 6,500rpm

Carburettors

Type	Amal 'Chopped' Monoblocs with fuel supply controlled by a shared Amal 14/617 float bowl
Choke size	$1\frac{1}{16}$in
Main jet	240
Pilot jet	25
Needle	Type C (third position)
Needle jet	0.1065

Fuel tank

Capacity	4 gallons (Imperial)

Gearbox (four speed)

top	4.57:1
3rd	5.45
2nd	7.75
1st	11.2

Electrics

Ignition	Lucas Magneto K2F 42298, manual advance
Charging circuit	Lucas Dynamo type E3L 6V, 60W output
Battery	6V, 12 ampere/hour PU7E9
Spark plugs	N3 gapped at 0.25

Tyres

Front	3.25 × 19in
Rear	3.50 × 19in

Brakes

Front	8in drum, single leading shoe
Rear	7in drum, single leading shoe

Engine and Early Problems

Having evolved from the Thunderbird via the Tiger 110, many design features of the Bonneville engine were shared, and some had been improved. The tried and trusted 360 degree, 649cc vertical twin followed conventional over-head valve layout using the E3134 inlet cam (first seen in 1952 as part of the Tiger 100 Race Kit) and E3225 exhaust camshafts. As with the rest of the Triumph twins, these camshafts ran in bush

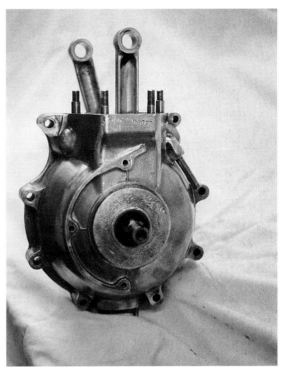

1960 650cc T120 pre-unit construction engine assembled and ready for installation.

Assembled crank, flywheel and con rods installed in crank case.

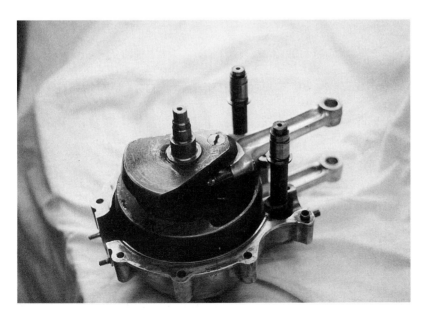

The one-piece forged EN16B crankshaft with straight-sided cheeks and bolt-on cast iron central flywheel secured by three radial bolts. The H section con rods were manufactured in RR56 alloy and had plain shell bearing big ends.

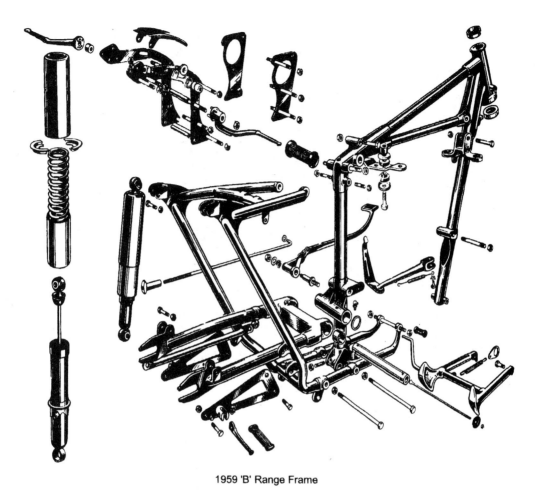

1959 'B' Range Frame

Shared with the T110, the original single downtube Bonneville chassis was of brazed tube construction and came equipped with an 'Easy lift' centre stand, an optional prop stand and provision for an anti-theft steering head lock.

bearings in the crankcase and were driven via an idler gear from a pinion on the right-hand side of the crankshaft. The exhaust cam was sited ahead of the cylinder block and the inlet cam behind. Each cam operated followers situated in blocks pressed into the bottom of the barrel castings. The cam followers activated alloy push rods housed within chromed steel tubes partially recessed within the engine finning and running vertically up to the rocker boxes, one in front of the cylinders and one behind. The valves ($1\frac{1}{2}$in inlet, $1\frac{1}{32}$in exhaust) were controlled by dual coil valve

springs. Each rocker could be accessed via a circular inspection cover threaded into the rocker boxes to enable valve clearance inspection and adjustment. The chromed steel push rod tubes were nominally sealed by square section neoprene 'O' ring oil seals.

The cylinder block was cast in one piece with an air gap between each barrel to help cool the cylinder bores. The base flange of the cylinder block was held by eight studs threaded into the crankcase and the die-cast alloy cylinder head was secured to the block by eight $\frac{3}{8}$in bolts.

Close up of the twin downtubes featured on the Duplex frame of the 1960 T120 Bonneville.

The Bonneville shared a one-piece crankshaft forging (EN16B) with the other 1959 650cc twins. Initial problems with flywheel bolt break-ages were solved by tightening the interference fit of the flywheel bore and corresponding crankshaft spigot diameter by 0.0025in. The flywheel was heated to 95°C before being fitted onto the crank. The assembly operation required deft handling by the fitter who had to wear a heavy pair of protec-tive gloves. As an additional precaution new fly-wheel bolts were fitted from engine number 027610 onwards. Two ball-race main bearings supported the crankshaft in the crankcase halves. H-section connecting rods made of RR56 alloy

were secured by high tensile stretch bolts that clamped a detachable shell bearing into the big end; plain bush bearings served at the small end.

The big end bearings were supplied with oil through a dry sump lubrication system. Drillings in the crankshaft were end-fed from oilways in the timing chest cover where plain bearings sup-ported the crankshaft nose and the camshaft drive idler pinion. An eccentric peg on the nut secur-ing the inlet camshaft pinion drove the double-plunger oil pump. A pressure relief valve with oil pressure indicator was positioned on the lower corner of the timing cover. After circulating, oil drained into the sump through a mesh strainer.

The mesh could be accessed via a rectangular sump plate beneath the crank case. From the sump, oil was scavenged back to the oil tank or, through a T-piece connector in the return pipe, to the rocker spindles.

Twin $1\frac{1}{16}$in Amal Monobloc carburettors were mounted on flanged inlet stubs which were screwed into the cylinder head via threaded inlet tracts. These stubs were locked into position with large locking nuts on the exposed section of thread. Unlike the prototype, on the first generation of production Bonnevilles the carburettors were modified to fit by having the float bowls removed. These 'chopped' carburettors were sited side by side beneath the tank and fuel supplied by a remote Amal 14/617 float chamber of the type used on the GP Competition 500. To prevent vibration causing aeration of the fuel, this float bowl was supported by a rubber mount secured on the frame's main downtube. Sadly, instead of aeration, this arrangement was prone to fuel surge problems under hard acceleration and by 1961 Triumph had followed the example set by many frustrated owners and installed standard, unchopped, Monoblocs which seemed to fit into the confined space after all.

The Bonneville's splayed port cylinder head was not a completely new component. The same casting had been used for the parallel port T110 head and traces of the original, undrilled induction tracts and the old cast number beneath the inlet rocker box remained. On the exhaust side, the exhaust downpipes were secured by finned ring clamps located over stubs cast into the head. Initially the same $1\frac{1}{2}$in straight-through exhausts as carried by the T110 were fitted, but with impending noise legislation looming, internally baffled O24337 silencers with the same outward appearance were specified.

The 8.5 to 1 compression ratio cast alloy pistons suffered from crown collapse under intense use, and consequently crown thickness was increased twice during the first year of manufacture. To avoid interruptions to production, manufacturing tolerances were maximized and adjustments made to the dimensions of the casting die during routine maintenance. To improve heat dissipation a similar alteration was made to the thickness of the piston skirt. Clearance between skirt and crankshaft bobweights was also increased. High performance pistons giving a 12 to 1 compression ratio were available, along with racing valve springs and guides.

In US competition use the gearbox camplate was seen to suffer premature wear. From engine number 023941 this was remedied by induction hardening the periphery of the plate, a solution that was also applied to the clutch sprocket centre. A more reliable voltage regulator was fitted. Spot welding the front mudguard blade to the central mounting bridge (engine number 021941 onwards) temporarily solved a vibration cracking problem, a snag that was to reappear in the Bonneville's later life.

Transmission and Gearing

Little on the Bonneville was completely new. Components had evolved by trial and gradual improvement, often over a period of many years. The Bonneville's gearbox was a prime example of that evolutionary development.

Sited behind the engine in its own alloy casing, the four-speed positive-stop selection gearbox was related directly to the original Speed Twin of 1938. Of conventional British design, with drive input and output on the left-hand side and the gear lever on the right, the Bonneville gearbox used the same mainshaft and layshaft pinions as the T110. The gear lever moved a quadrant which acted upon a centrally mounted camplate. A track in this camplate engaged with rollers on two selector forks which ran on a shared spindle to move pinions on their shafts. At the bottom of the gearbox casing, a spring-loaded plunger engaged with indentations on the edge of the camplate to provide positive indexing of the gears. Later (*see* above) this camplate edge was induction hardened to cope with the rigours of US desert racing.

To help transmit the increased power produced by the Bonnie the five driven plates of the clutch were fitted with Neolangite friction material bearing on six plain steel driving plates. Four adjustable coil springs provided pressure on the plates which ran in a clutch drum driven by a 70 link $\frac{1}{2}$in × $\frac{5}{16}$in single row Renold primary chain lubricated by a $\frac{1}{4}$ pint of SAE 20 oil. The primary drive cover was secured by longer screws from engine number 022861 onwards.

At the clutch centre, rubber inserts surrounding a vaned paddle drive absorbed transmission shocks that would otherwise be conducted from the engine mainshaft. The clutch sprocket centre bore was induction hardened from engine number 024029.

The primary chain was tensioned by pivoting the gearbox on the lower of its mounts using an adjuster fitted to the upper mount (from engine number 023111 an additional adjuster was used for this). The final drive chain could then be adjusted as required by moving the rear wheel in the frame.

Rear Frame

Triumph's 650 had first been fitted with swinging arm rear suspension in 1954 when the Tiger 110 appeared. The 1959 Bonneville's frame was the same as that of the T110. Made in traditional style with frame tubes brazed into cast lugs the 1959 frame had a single front downtube with separate front and rear frame sections bolted together at the top of the seat post and below the swinging arm pivot. The swinging arm was of the same tubular construction and pivoted on metal Oilite bushes. The Girling rear suspension units were fitted with hydraulically damped springs rated at 100lb/in. The pre-loading of the springs could be adjusted but the damping was fixed. The upper shrouds were finished in black and the lower chrome plated. Various spring ratings, ranging from 150lb/in for sidecar use to 90lb/in for racing units, could be specified by the customer.

Steering and Front Forks

Cup-and-cone ball bearings were used in the steering head to mount conventional internally sprung telescopic front forks. Different spring ratings were identified by spots of coloured paint. Red signified the standard solo-rated springs and blue spots identified those for sidecar use. Springs

marked with purple were for extra heavy sidecar use.

Bonnevilles manufactured for the home market were equipped with low swept-back handlebars. Those intended for the US market were fitted with wider high-rise bars. Both types were secured in semi-circular recesses in the cast iron top yoke by steel u-bolts fixed with $\frac{5}{16}$in nuts and spring washers. Handlebars for the UK and general export markets were subsequently changed to a straighter sports style. Optional dropped road-racing handlebars featuring a special bend that allowed them to be fitted around the nacelle were available. These bars were of a smaller $\frac{7}{8}$in diameter and required shims to be fitted in the handlebar clamps and $\frac{7}{8}$in controls and grips. The old-fashioned two-piece pressed steel nacelle suited neither the sports bars nor the high-level US handlebars and was soon deleted from the Bonneville's specification.

Early, pre-production, photographs show Bonnevilles for the UK market fitted with a pressed steel clutch and brake lever without the ball-end safety feature. By the launch date, ball-ended levers were a standard fitment.

The handlebar grips had the Triumph name moulded into the rubber and on the left-hand side of the handlebars the combined horn/dip switch was fixed by a saddle clamp. Also on the left, inboard of the dip switch, was an ignition advance/retard lever.

The friction steering damper mounted beneath the bottom fork yoke was adjusted by a black enamelled knob mounted centrally on the nacelle.

Wheels, Tyres and Brakes

Like the frame, Bonneville also shared its 8in full-width front hub and brake drum with the T110. The hub ran on two ball races, the left bearing held by a circlip and the right secured by a retaining ring which screwed into the hub with a left-hand thread. This right-hand bearing also located against a backing ring which engaged with a shoulder on the wheel spindle.

The brake was a single-leading-shoe assembly mounted on a polished alloy backplate. A slot cast in its outer face located on an anchoring tongue on the right fork leg. Brake linings were rivetted to the shoes which had return springs operating at both the fulcrum and the operating cam ends. The operating lever was located on a square shanked operating cam and itself had a return spring working against a locating hole in the back plate. If properly serviced, the front brake provided adequate stopping power, but a careful view of the road well ahead had to be maintained if the bike was ridden at speed.

On the left side of the hub a circular cover plate was fitted. Early covers had a radial pattern pressed into them but later types used the same plain plate as the T110. Forty $8/10G \times 5\frac{5}{8}$in straight-pull spokes laced the hub into a chromium-plated 19in WM2-19 rim fitted with a ribbed 3.25×19in Dunlop tyre.

At the rear, either a standard or a Quickly Detachable (QD) wheel option could be chosen. The standard fitment had a 7in cast iron brake drum with a 46-tooth final drive sprocket cut into its outer edge. Eight bolts secured by paired tab washers held the brake drum/sprocket to the hub. Like the front hub, the rear hub ran on two ballraces and housed a single-leading-shoe brake mounted on a pressed steel back plate. Each end of the wheel spindle carried an adjuster for setting chain tension and wheel alignment.

The QD option provided a rear wheel running on three bearings. Two Timken taper-roller bearings were contained within the hub and the centre of the brake drum was supported by a ball race. The hub was splined into the brake drum to allow the wheel to be removed without dismantling the brake assembly or disturbing the adjustment of the drive chain. By simply undoing and withdrawing the wheel spindle and spacer from the right-hand side the wheel could be lifted from the frame leaving the brake drum/sprocket fixed securely in situ on its ballrace. The QD wheel made changing or repairing tyres much easier and was consequently a popular fitment. Whether QD or bolt up, Bonneville rear wheels were fitted with $8/10G \times 8$in spokes on the left side and $8/10G \times 8\frac{3}{8}$in on the right. All had 90 degree heads and were laced into a WM2-19 chromed steel rim fitted with a 3.50×19in Dunlop Universal tyre.

Cycle Parts and Fittings

Most controversial feature of the new Bonneville was the styling of the cycle parts. Clearly, the rush to include the new Bonneville in the 1959 line-up had resulted in many Tiger 110 components being utilized. The consequent compromise meant the sports Bonneville became loaded with heavy, touring type, equipment.

Along with the dissonant nacelle, the deeply valanced mudguards proved especially unpopular in the United States. The heavy front mudguard was secured to the fork legs by a substantial stay which also provided support for the front of the bike when the front wheel was removed. Two short pieces of strip steel were rivetted to the mudguard at its mid-section to provide a fixing higher up the fork. These early rivetted joints suffered vibration cracks and later mudguards had welded top fixings. To provide additional rigidity, the mudguard edges were rolled and each had a raised strip running along the centre. The centre strip was painted and lined, with the resulting coloured stripe finishing short of the rolled edge of the mudguard. On the front guard this centre strip carried a number plate mounted in its aluminium frame – strange but standard equipment for a sports bike intended for US export, where no front number was required.

The welded-steel petrol tank equipped with distinctive Triumph grille badges and parcel grid had long been a prominent feature of the Triumph range. UK models received a 4 gallon version whilst US machines were fitted with 3 gallon (Imperial) capacity tanks with a filler cap on a retaining chain, as on the Trophy. Rubber knee pads were fitted to both types of tank but the smaller US tank had smaller pads held by mounting plates. The larger UK knee pads screwed directly onto the tank. Each tank was equipped with two petrol taps, one on each side at the rear.

A 5 pint oil tank was mounted beneath the seat on the right side of the machine, painted black for UK and general export but finished in 'pearl grey' for the United States. Later, UK models were also given coloured oil tanks. On the other side of the bike the oil tank was balanced by a tool box and battery cover painted to match.

The tool kit contained a magneto spanner, clutch hub extractor, screwdrivers and a range of spanners. The tool box cover was held by a single large screw and could be readily removed with the edge of a large coin.

Seat

An early Bonneville fitment was the Tiger 110 two-level dual seat. This was soon replaced by the more spartan single-level item specified for the Trophy. Slimmer and with less padding, the Trophy seat was more in keeping with the Bonneville's sports styling. Both of the seats used during the first model year were upholstered in black Vynide, with white piping for the original 'wide' T110 type and with a grey trim around the bottom edge of the slimmer Trophy sports version.

Electrics and Speedometer

In keeping with the Bonneville's sporting image, the Lucas K2F magneto with manually controlled ignition timing was fitted. Situated behind the cylinder block the magneto was secured to the inner face of the timing chest by three special $\frac{5}{16}$in nuts made to accept the smaller $\frac{1}{4}$in spanner size. The drive shaft projected into the timing chest where the magneto pinion engaged with the inlet camshaft gear. By adjusting the pinion on the magneto's tapered drive shaft, timing could be set at the specified fully advanced position of 39 degrees (or $\frac{7}{16}$in) before top dead centre (BTDC). Contact-breaker points were set at 0.012in when fully open. The manual advance and retard lever was mounted on the left handlebar. The various fitments of KLG FE100, Lodge HLN or Champion N3 spark plugs were all gapped at 0.020in.

Auto-advance units for the Lucas K2 magneto range were introduced later that year. US models were equipped with Lucas's K2FC Red Label competition magneto or the ultimate sports option, the K2FR racing magneto which could be specially ordered by the most demanding customers.

Lights and horn on the T120 were powered by a 6V, 12 ampere/hour Lucas PU7E/9 battery. The 7in Lucas headlamp was equipped with a pre-focus 30/24W bulb made to dip left for UK use or a 35/35W straight dip for the US market. The headlamp also carried a 3W pilot lamp. Behind the red lens on the rear number plate mount was a 6/18W stop and tail lamp bulb. A spring-loaded switch operated by the rear brake pedal controlled the stop light. The positive-earth electrical system was charged by a 6V Lucas E3L-L10 dynamo strapped to the front of the crankcase and driven by a pinion meshing with the exhaust cam drive gear. The dynamo produced 60W with the output controlled by a Lucas RB107 regulator. After engine number 024137 a Lucas 37725H regulator was used. Charging and battery condition could be monitored using the Lucas ammeter mounted on the left of the nacelle. The light switch was on the right of the nacelle and the engine kill switch button lay centrally between them.

The 120mph Smith's Chronometric speedometer was mounted prominently in the nacelle and driven by cable from a pinion on the end of the gearbox layshaft. An optional tachometer was available.

Although the dubious 'tangerine' and 'pearl grey' colour scheme had startled even US customers (to the extent that the 'tangerine' tanks of left over 1959 machines could be seen dotting the forecourts of American dealerships well into 1960), Triumph had achieved its intention. The bike had made a creditable impression during its first year and was well received. By 1960 the Bonneville was looking forward to a long and successful production run. Few realized just how long that run would be.

1960 – THE STATE OF THE INDUSTRY

During 1960 Gary Richards clocked 149.51mph (240.56km/h) on an unfaired T120 Bonneville.

Suzuki and Honda entered the Isle of Man TT races. Honda secured positions in the first ten in both the 125cc and 250cc events.

Triumph's 1960 Earl's Court stand exhibited a Speed Twin with an electric starter, a feature intended for British police bike production.

Parent group BSA made a record profit of £3.5m. Triumph production policy and decision making became increasingly subject to BSA management input.

T120 Bonneville 1960

Price: £284 13s 6d
Commencing engine number 029424 and D101

Frame

Some regarded the 1959 Bonnie to be more representative of a final version of the Tiger 110 than the first of a new range of machines, so radical were the changes made to the 1960 Bonneville. For the new season, Triumph addressed the Bonneville's high-speed handling problems. The single downtube T110 frame had been a compromise forced by the urgency of the previous year's launch. Within months of that launch the Bonneville's performance and the sporting aspirations of many riders showed that a fundamentally revised chassis was needed, not only to prevent high-speed weave and wobble, but also to allow scope for the inevitable further development of the engine.

Other than the black enamel finish, little of the old T110 frame was carried over to the 1960

1960 – Turner Visits Japan

Keen to monitor international developments in the business and aware that the winds of competition would soon blow from the East, Edward Turner toured Japan. Although already familiar with the products of Honda, Yamaha and Suzuki, Turner was shocked by the total commitment to quality shown in the Japanese factories. He noted that Japan was already the largest manufacturer of motorcycles in the world and the awesome fact that any single Japanese company could produce more than the whole British motorcycle industry of that time. Total annual Japanese output was well over 500,000 machines, compared with Britain's 140,000.

His visits to the Japanese manufacturing plants gave stark confirmation of their potential production capacity. At Honda he found a factory able to produce 1,000 commuter motorcycles per day, equivalent to more than a week's production in any UK factory existing at that time. He recognized that economies of scale well beyond the levels of UK production would clearly favour Japanese manufacturers as output grew in the future; he considered that the situation for the UK industry was already bad and, as the market expanded, it could only get worse.

He found the level of Japanese resources devoted to research and development startling, a stark demonstration of the progressive Japanese manufacturing policy that was designed to prevent models ranges stagnating.

Turner found readily available, well educated, skilled staff accommodated in company-owned houses with subsidised rent. They were able to buy food and domestic consumables at cost price through the company store and, once on the company pay-roll, established staff were retained through good times and bad. Social responsibilities were recognized and filled by the company in order to ensure worker loyalty.

Turner concluded that the British industry had to recognize that both its home and export markets were at risk. Well-equipped machines were flooding off Japanese production lines and cost 20 per cent less than an equivalent British bike. The scale of Japanese manufacturing not only produced quality motorcycles at affordable prices, but also created wealth on a global scale. This gave more people the purchasing power to buy and so generated more customers, thus giving a virtuous circle of wealth creation producing potential buyers as well as machines.

Shaken by the menace of Japanese manufacturing, Turner was prepared to think the unthinkable, even considering the opening of a Japanese plant and the shifting of production.

In the end senior management in the motorcycle industry adopted the misguided, but temporarily reassuring, belief that customers would progress from their small Japanese-manufactured bikes to more worthwhile British machines. In Britain, few believed this situation could last, even if it had ever existed; in Japan, nobody paused to consider the idea.

Bonneville. The solution to the early handling problem was increased rigidity. On the new bike this was to be provided by a completely updated duplex frame.

Fitted from engine number 029364 to 030424 and D101 onwards, the new frame featured twin downtubes which dropped from the steering head, curved under the engine to join the rear subframe at a substantial new lug at the bottom of the vertical seatpost. The new downtubes provided an instant distinguishing feature for the new model, but more significantly, when combined with the strengthened rear subframe, they transformed the bike's handling. This stronger and shorter rear subframe was now of welded construction with a longer rear loop to provide support for the rear mudguard. To improve handling still further, the steering head angle

was increased from 64.5 degrees to 67 degrees. This reduced the bike's wheelbase from $55\frac{3}{4}$in to $54\frac{1}{2}$in.

One retrograde feature of the duplex frame was the omission of a lower tank rail. Under the extreme conditions of American desert racing, the twin downtubes beneath the steering head lug could flex and eventually break. The breakages would become a severe problem and, under racing conditions, could prove fatal. To counter this, a lower tank rail or secondary cross bar was included in a revised front frame section fitted from engine number D1536 onwards. Many dealers retro-fitted this new front section to strengthen older machines. Belatedly, it was also realized that changes to the frame geometry and the use of stiffer springs in the front forks meant that the prop stand was too short to support the bike safely. It was modified midseason.

Front Forks and Steering

Apart from handling, a secondary consideration had been the conflict between the bike's obvious sporting potential and the staid touring-style equipment with which it was fitted. Changes were afoot. For the 1960 model the nacelle was discarded and instead a TR6 Trophy top yoke was exposed to view. Black fork shrouds carrying headlamp brackets supported a sporty chrome headlamp shell. Without the old-fashioned nacelle the speedometer and optional tachometer could be mounted as a matched pair on the top yoke above the headlamp. Below the headlamp rubber gaiters protected front forks that were now damped for both shock and rebound. The handlebars were secured by bolt-on caps and mounting clamps that were raised and extended back behind the trailing edge of the yoke.

Electrics

From 1960 all Bonnevilles were fitted with alternator-fed electrical systems. The Lucas RM15 6V alternator was mounted within the primary drive chaincase on the left-hand end of the crankshaft. This charged the same 12ampare/ hour Lucas PU7E/9 battery fitted the previous year through an AC/DC rectifier. Performance of the system

The single downtube frame of the original 1959 model.

The 1960 version of the T120 Bonneville; removal of the nacelle and the deeply valanced front mudguard transformed the bike's appearance.

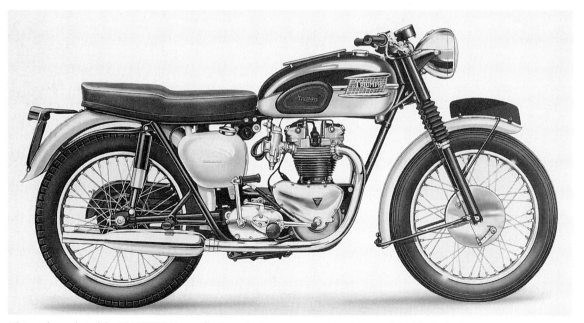

This catalogue shot of the 1960 T120 Bonneville shows the leaner, more sporting, character of the bike beginning to appear.

The 1960 T120 Bonneville, pre-unit construction, duplex frame and separate chrome-plated headlamp shell.

could be monitored via the ammeter mounted on the headlamp shell. After the removal of the dreaded nacelle the light switch had to be resited on the right-hand side panel of the bike, beneath the nose of a new split-level dual seat. The Smith's 140mph Chronometric speedometer was bracketed to the top yoke ahead of the steering damper knob and the engine cut-out was positioned to the right of the damper. Also muffled away under the seat was a means of giving almost audible warning of approach, the Lucas 6V horn.

With the adoption of an automatic advance unit on the Lucas K2F Magneto the manual advance/retard control was removed from the left handlebar. US-export models continued to benefit from auto advance on the K2FC compe-

tition equivalent. A new Type 6A brake light switch was fitted.

The principal change to the wiring loom was the provision of a quick release plug and socket connection to the headlamp shell, but as a result Lucas was awarded the honorary title of 'Prince of Darkness' by many Triumph riders. In service the plug loosened and often left riders travelling at speed in the pitch black whilst groping for the brake lever. In spite of this, the feature was retained until 1962.

Engine

The fitting of the new alternator meant that a new bulkier primary chaincase was needed. This in turn required a modification to the left-hand exhaust pipe where it passed the alternator bulge. The exhaust system remained 1½in in diameter and gained removable baffles in the silencers. US-export TR7B off-roaders were fitted with high-level exhausts with protective heat shields and TR7A roadsters received an exhaust cam driven tachometer as standard. This tacho drive required a new timing cover with repositioned Triumph patent plate.

Fuel Supply and Carburettors

To combat early fuel surge and frothing problems, the remote float chamber was reconfigured for 1960. Instead of mounting the Type 14/617 float chamber ahead of the toolbox, a Type 14/624 remote float chamber was suspended from a threaded rod fitted to a metalastic mounting on the cylinder head torque steady plate. This positioned the float bowl assembly further forward than previously (it now lay hidden and inaccessible between the carburettors) but did little to cure the fuel frothing problem. The final, and perhaps rather too obvious, solution proved to be the fitting of standard Amal Monoblocs complete with their integral float bowls. This was applied from engine number D5975.

Transmission and Gearing

The engine sprocket was reduced from 24 to 22 teeth resulting in a reduction in overall gearing.

Cycle Parts and Fittings

The lean and hungry sports look was extended to the mudguards which lost their heavy side valences. The front wheel was screened by a narrow painted alloy blade (albeit still supported by a heavy stay which continued to double as the front wheel stand) and the rear wheel was shielded by a slimmer steel mudguard. Both had straight cut leading and trailing edges and consequently the painted centre stripes extended right up to the end of the blade. Traditionally, on Triumph mudguards manufactured with rolled edges the painted stripe finished before reaching the end of the blade.

A new split-level dual seat with a little extra padding now eased the rider's progress. Covered in black vinyl with white piping and a black lower rim trim the new seat was bolted, not hinged, to the frame. The fuel tank was secured by a chromed steel strap lined with rubber that lay along the centre seam of the tank. This pulled the tank down onto three rubber mounts, two at the front, one at the rear. A rubber collar under the tank located against the frame top tube to give lateral support. From engine number D104, the factory supplied specially produced rubber blocks to provide this sideways support. The tank strap was tensioned by a draw bolt tightened against the lower frame lug on the steering head. As before, UK bikes were equipped with a 4 gallon fuel tank and US models received the 3 Imperial gallon size. All carried the chromed parcel rack.

Colours for the 1960 Bonneville were 'pearl

Detailed rear quarter view of a 1960 T120 Bonnie, frequently the only view riders of lesser machines were permitted as the Triumph accelerated past.

Taking pride of place in John Newton's Triumph collection, shown here in 1983, was his 1960 T120 Bonneville. Left to right, T120 Bonneville, T110 and Speed Twin.

Initially rebuilt to 1961 UK spec, this T120 Bonneville belongs to Mike Poynton of Stockport. Detailed research revealed the bike's actual date of manufacture to be 23 May 1960 and resulted in a new paint job and the fitting of the correct, 1960 specification, black top seat.

The age-related NFF 347 license number allocated to Mike's 1960 T120 is the machine's first UK registration. The bike returned from the United States in March 1993.

Close up of the drive side of Mike's T120 crankcase prior to the initial rebuild. Factory records show the bike, T120 D6073, to have been a US-export model manufactured in May of 1960.

grey' and 'azure blue' with gold lining around the coloured stripe on mudguards and the colour division on the tank. The oil tank and battery box were painted 'pearl grey'.

At last the Bonneville was finding a coherent theme. Sporting potential was being matched with lightweight fittings that gave the bike a purposeful appearance and greater customer appeal. In keeping with the bike's sporting image, the sharper, starkly functional, style would be further refined and remain the bike's style for the next two decades of production.

In America, to distinguish the new season's stock from leftover 1959 'tangerine dream' T120's, the duplex-framed 1960 model was designated the Triumph TR7A (roadster) and the TR7B (off-road version). However, the distinction was needed only temporarily; once the glut of 1959 machines was absorbed by the market, the TR7 coding became obsolete. The engine number prefix of all 1959 and 1960 models remained as T120.

1961 – THE STATE OF THE INDUSTRY

Gary Richards pushed his unfaired T120 Bonneville 10mph faster and clocked 159.54mph (256.70km/h).

For the American market the T120R (road) and T120C (competition) models were introduced. Different specifications were made available to suit the distinct preferences of US East and West Coast customers. The T120C was later developed by Johnson Motors into the T120C TT Special off-road racer for release in 1963.

Bert Hopwood returned to Triumph as Director and General Manager in May 1961. Design engineer and long-time motorcycle industry insider, he later proposed a three-cylinder Trident prototype. Development engineer Doug Hele (ex-Norton) completed drawings for the bike the following year.

Jack Sangster retired at the age of 65.

T120 Bonneville 1961

Price: £288 5s 11d
Commencing engine number D7727

Cycle Parts and Fittings
For 1961, a new welded steel fuel tank with reinforced nose bridge piece was mounted on three

The reinforced 1961 duplex frame showing the lower tank rail.

rubber feet and secured a rubber-lined stainless steel strap (short for the small US tank, longer for the UK) running centrally over the tank from front to back. The stainless steel straps proved stronger than the plated version and, after a series of five changes in design and material, eventually ended the previous year's problem of strap breakages. New colours for the petrol tank were a 'sky blue' top with a silver lower half separated by gold lining. To counter vibration cracking, a rubber-mounted oil tank was introduced. Sports-type mudguards front and rear were coloured silver with 'sky blue' stripe and gold lining.

Engine
The only change was to the cylinder head casting. To deaden cylinder block ringing, vertical pillars were introduced to brace the outer cooling fins.

Frame
The only change to the frame was the steering head angle, which was altered to 65 degrees.

Fuel Supply and Carburettors
Standard monoblocs continued to be fitted.

Electrics and Speedometer
Alternator output was reduced in an attempt to prevent bulb failures at high engine speeds. A Type 22B brake light switch was fitted along with auto-advance ignition. However, it was still not possible to vary ignition timing independently on each cylinder, and thus only a mean optimum ignition timing could be achieved.

Transmission and Gearing
The multi-plate clutch was improved with Langite non-stick friction lining. The needle roller layshaft bearings, main casing and inner cover were modified to accept larger thrust washers at each end of the layshaft. The engine sprocket was reduced from 22 to 21 teeth. The gearbox ratios were reduced, further lowering the overall gearing.

A modified 1961 Bonneville at rest in a rural setting. The Thruxton front pipes are after-market additions.

1961 T120 Bonneville, but fitted with non-standard Amal Concentric carburettors. Monoblocs were the standard fitment until 1967.

John Stracey hurls his 650cc pre-unit construction Bonneville into a right hander during the 1962 Thruxton 500.

Rear Suspension

Girling hydraulically damped suspension units were fitted, with spring rates of 100lb/in.

Wheels, Tyres and Brakes

The rear tyre was now a 4.00 section Dunlop Universal fitted to a wider WM3-18 rim. New brake back plates and fully floating shoes were provided. This fully floating front brake shoe arrangement was a standard fitment until 1966.

1962 – THE STATE OF THE INDUSTRY

Bert Hopwood proposed the production of a range of modular engine units; in other words, established and proven cylinder and valve gear units offering optimum performance that could be assembled into single, twin, triple and four-cylinder engines. This design approach would be a move towards the application of the 'maximum commonality of parts and tools' policy long advocated

Ned Minihan riding his 649cc Triumph Bonneville T120 in the 1962 Thruxton 500. The increased rigidity of the duplex frame solved the handling problems of the earliest Bonnevilles which had used the single downtube Tiger 110 chassis.

by Hopwood. To be commercially viable, this manufacturing policy would have to be applied to substantially increased production levels.

Bill Johnson, a trucker based in Los Angeles (not Bill Johnson of the US Triumph dealers Johnson Motors) set a new world speed record of 224.57mph (361.33km/h). Using a 649cc streamliner built by Joe Dudek, Johnson's two-way trip across Bonneville's salt was properly observed by an authorized FIM timekeeper. At last Triumph had secured an officially recognized world record. Johnson's record attempt very nearly ended in disaster when his machine went into a life-threatening 200mph swerve.

Triumph won the Daytona 200 mile Classic.

The unproven Tina scooter was launched without sufficient pre-production development, a possible early sign of management trouble ahead.

Home-grown lightweights the BSA Beagle and Ariel Pixie were offered at the 1962 Earl's Court Show. Unfortunately, dealers and, more importantly, customers were decidedly unimpressed.

Doug Hele and the Meriden development shop gave the Bonneville an increased fork trail and stiffer rear fork pivot, which radically improved handling. A rubber-mounted Bonneville oil tank cured its seam splitting problem.

Percy Tait riding his T110 in the 1956 Thruxton 500; note the single carburettor.

All Triumph 650cc twins produced after October 1962 were manufactured in unit construction form.

Approximately 350 machines were being produced at Meriden each week. Although dealers were unable to get enough machines to satisfy customer demand, factory output was not, or perhaps more accurately could not be, increased.

T120 Bonneville 1962

Price: £295 1s 4d
Commencing engine number D15789
Models: T120, T120R and T120C

Engine

To provide greater precision when setting valve timing, three keyway slots were provided on the cam wheel pinions. This provided improved sequencing of the E3134 inlet and E3325 exhaust camshafts. This modification, previously seen as a specialist racing tweak, was now assimilated into standard road-going specifications.

The EN16B crankshaft, fitted with a bolt-on central flywheel providing a balance factor of 71 per cent, started the year with engine number D15789, but after engine number D17043 it was superseded by the introduction of a pear-shaped web flywheel and crankshaft assembly.

Thruxton again, this time in 1959, with Tony Godfrey riding an early Bonneville. Although ready to race, the twin carbed T120 retains the heavily valanced touring mudguards and nacelle beneath the sporting flyscreen and competition number plates.

Although heavier, and introducing a consequent delay in throttle response, this pear-shaped web flywheel gave an improved balance factor of 85 per cent, reduced engine vibration and provided racers with a better 'bite' as the machine hit the ground after the aerobatics common in American-style TT enduro and moto-cross events.

Fuel Supply
The carburettors were left unchanged but new style 'gas' type fuel taps were connected to allow one tap to feed both carburettors and provide a reserve supply controlled by the other tap should one half of the tank run dry. This was a sound idea in principle, but in spirited use both taps had to be wide open to prevent fuel starvation.

Cycle Parts and Fittings
The new seat for 1962 had a Latex foam cushion with grey Vynide top panel, white piping, black sides and grey lower rim trim. It had the same seat base and mounting as used in the previous year. The new model had painted steel mudguards

Norton frame, pre-unit construction Bonneville engine and gearbox; the essential ingredients of a typical Triton in clubman competition trim.

Extensive use was made of the pre-unit construction Bonneville engine and gearbox in road and race specials. Here is a very well turned out Triton, Norton frame powered by a Triumph engine.

front and rear. The oil tank and toolbox was now black for UK and general export. Updated colours, available in the US only, were 'silver sheen' and 'flame' with gold lining.

Ignition, Lighting and Speedometer
The 140mph speedometer was made a standard fitting. The unreliable headlamp plug and socket QD facility was finally deleted on safety grounds.

Rear Suspension
Girling hydraulic damper units were fitted with 145lb/in. springs.

Transmission and Gearing
A higher third gear gearbox ratio was specified.

7 Unit Construction Bonnevilles

1963 – THE STATE OF THE INDUSTRY

The parent group BSA closed the Ariel factory at Selly Oak, Birmingham. Norton's factory at Bracebridge Street, Birmingham was also closed.

Hopwood and Hele made the first sketches of the production version of the three-cylinder 750cc engine for the Trident.

The 1957 348cc 3TA Twenty One led the way into unit construction. The name of this bike celebrated the twenty-one years that had elapsed since the 1936 revitalization of the Triumph Engineering Company, and conveniently coincided with the 21cu.in displacement of the bike's engine, as quoted on the American market. When the Bonneville eventually followed in 1963 the only surprise was why the adoption of unit construction for the rest of the Triumph range had taken so long. On purely economic grounds, unit construction of the Bonneville's engine and gearbox was inevitable.

With the change to unit construction

The earliest unit construction Triumph, the 1957 348cc 3TA 'Twenty One'.

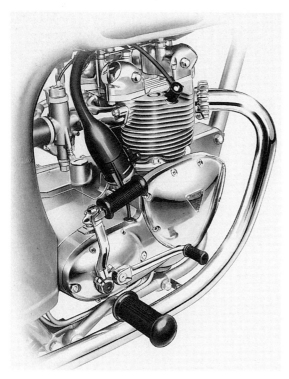

The 1957 348cc 3TA Twenty One had led the way into unitized construction of the engine and gearbox as a single assembly. When the Bonneville eventually followed the same design practice in 1963 the only surprise was why the adoption of unit construction for the rest of the Triumph range had taken so long.

Bonneville embarked upon a period of prolonged and remorseless development intended to keep the bike ahead in an increasingly competitive market. As with previous changes, the alterations were carefully managed. The technical innovation and improvement necessary were successfully implemented without loss of the Bonnie's essential sporting character. From the factory's point of view, there were other significant benefits. Whilst increased performance and reliability were the declared aims of the continued development programme, reduced cost of manufacture could also be addressed. The simplified procedure required to assemble and install a single engine/gearbox unit offered economy of effort at the manufacturing stage.

The resulting cost benefit could be passed on to the customer or retained as an additional element of profit.

T120 Bonneville 1963

Price: £318
Commencing engine number DU101
Models: T120, T120R and T120C

Engine

With the appearance of the DU unit construction engine number prefix the Bonneville's motor underwent fundamental change. The engine, gearbox and primary drive were rationalized into a single unit with a duplex-chain primary drive. The heavy and vulnerable magneto was replaced by a compact twin-contact breaker coil ignition, the eight cylinder head bolts were rearranged diametrically outwards and a central, ninth, $\frac{5}{16}$in bolt was added to ensure that an adequate gas seal was maintained between the cylinders. This rearrangement provided more clearance around the valves and, by virtue of improved heat dissipation, reduced the likelihood of cracks around the valve seats, a prevalent failing of the previous eight-bolt cylinder head. Additionally, although valve sizes remained unchanged for the time being, the greater clearance allowed by the bolt rearrangement provided scope for later increases in valve diameter. Below the head a new nine-stud cylinder block accommodated the old 8.5 to 1 compression ratio pistons and connecting rods.

The rocker boxes now carried improved, horizontal finning and new, slightly shallower, cross-slotted tappet inspection caps. These were retained by spring steel clips bearing on the cap's serrated edges to prevent vibration-induced rotation and consequent loss of the cap.

Revised exhausts contained longer baffles and therefore gained a slightly heavier appearance. The high pipes fitted to US export T120C off-road models required only minimal change.

Styling of the new unit-construction bottom

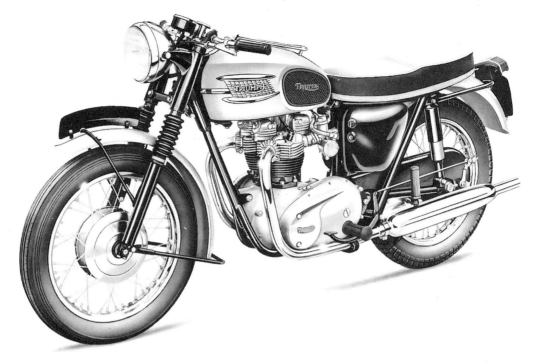

650 c.c. TRIUMPH BONNEVILLE 120 (T120)

The 1963 T120 650cc Bonneville in its home market guise. Fundamental design changes had taken place with the switch to unit construction of the engine and gearbox.

The East Coast version of the T120C Bonnie of 1963 as retailed by the Triumph Corporation of America.

end castings was carefully calculated to maintain the appearance of the old Bonneville. The contours of the old separate gearbox casing were echoed in the shape of the new integral gearbox cover with similar sympathetic regard being paid to the timing cover and the shortened primary chaincase.

Within the engine, more changes had been implemented. Beneath the triangular Triumph patent plate on the timing cover, wider pinions now drove E4819 inlet and E4855 exhaust camshafts. The left-hand end of the exhaust camshaft was equipped to take a tachometer drive cable. A new plunger oil pump fed lubricant from its right-hand chamber to the crankshaft's oilway on the timing-side end. Where previously the crankshaft nose had been fitted with a plain phosphor-bronze bush it now rotated in a proper oil seal, maintaining pressure in spite of milage and consequent wear. The oil pressure indicator was resited to face forwards on the front of the right-hand crankcase. The crankshaft/flywheel assembly's peripheral retaining bolts were made fast with Loctite fluid instead of serrated lock washers.

Transmission and Gearing

Behind the bold Triumph flash cast into the primary-drive cover lay new, stronger clutch springs, an additional friction plate and a $\frac{3}{8}$in. pitch duplex primary-drive chain driven by a 29-tooth engine sprocket. Because of the heavier clutch action resulting from the stronger springs acting on the six friction plates, an improved ball-and-ramp lifting mechanism was fitted in the unit gearbox outer cover. A 58-tooth cast iron clutch drum quietened by a bronze thrust washer fed power to the gearbox input shaft through a three-vane clutch centre shock absorber. Primary chain tension was maintained by a rubber-covered blade operating against the lower run. The gearbox sprocket carried 19 teeth and the rear wheel sprocket/break drum casting had 46 teeth. At the rear of the primary chaincase an oiler tube and metering jet ensured adequate lubrication of the rear chain.

Problems with Unit Construction

Along with the many changes in specification came a few in-service snags. Difficulty when selecting fourth gear was identified as a clearance problem between the unit construction gearbox shell and the gear selector quadrant. In the primary-drive chaincase a minor snag was associated with the clutch centre cushdrive rubbers. To soften these drive-line shock absorbers, rubber inserts with $\frac{1}{4}$in holes through the centres were fitted. In use they were found to break up and render the cushdrive ineffective. The solution was to replace these pierced inserts with rubber of a softer mix, this time moulded with chamfered edges. To identify the softer inserts the material was coloured green. A problem was also found when locating the steering lock nose in the crown stem.

These were all minor issues. Of greater concern was the occasional failure of the drive-side main bearing, possibly due to the stiffer and therefore less forgiving bearing location characteristics of the unit construction crankcase. To counter this, looser fitting '3 spot' (increased clearance) bearings were specified to reduce pre-loading stresses when the bearings were fitted into the new crankcase casting.

Even a change in the ignition system presented problems. The introduction of coil ignition was found to be the cause of high piston crown temperature and piston skirt seizure. Although the contact points could be accurately timed when the bike was in a brand new condition, as the fibre heel of the contact breaker points bedded down in use it became increasingly difficult to achieve the correct ignition timing on both cylinders without compromising the contact breaker points gap. Because this subtle finessing of timing against gap ultimately proved to be beyond the average owner, even sometimes beyond the average mechanic, many Bonnevilles were run with asymmetrical timing, in other words, one cylinder was correct while the other was nearly correct; or even worse, not quite right. The incorrect cylinder suffered as a result. To make matters worse, the timing inaccuracy on badly set-up bikes greatly increased the inherent vibration and consequently mud-guards, oil tanks and other fittings sustained vibration-related fractures. This problem was not resolved until 1967 when a redesigned contact breaker base plate allowed each of the rocker arms to be adjusted separately and thus enabled the correct and independent timing of both cylinders.

Performance Parts

The following performance parts were available:

- 8.5:1 compression ratio pistons machined to accommodate $\frac{3}{32}$in oversize valves, deeper D/24 compression and oil control piston rings, larger valve seats.
- Cylinder head with $1\frac{1}{8}$in. diameter inlet ports, carburettor adaptors and oversize valve seats.
- Nimonic exhaust valves.
- E2879 double-lipped roller main bearings, $1\frac{1}{8}$ in.
- Type 389 Amal carburettor and 14/624 remote float chamber.
- E3134 camshaft and followers, close ratio gears and appropriate speedometer drive gear.

Heavy-duty clutch springs, MZ41 racing brake linings and competition number plates were featured on the special performance parts list for 1963.

Cycle Parts and Fittings

The petrol tank was now secured by two rubber front mounts and a rubber bushed screw passing through a flat tab protruding at the rear of the tank into a threaded hole in the frame. The tank's capacity was slightly reduced due to the fabricated cut-aways in the underside which housed the twin ignition coils. A new rear mudguard was introduced to suit the updated rear subframe. Colours for 1963 were black oil tank, switch panel, frame, forks and fittings, with 'Alaskan white' petrol tank and white mudguards with gold centre stripe separated by black lining.

Frame

With the unit construction engine came a different frame. A single $1\frac{5}{8}$in diameter downtube and stronger 65 degree steering head casting featured at the front, whilst at the rear a swinging arm lug and stiffer rear engine plate arrangement gave the frame greatly increased lateral rigidity. A stronger swinging arm and easy-lift centre stand were standard equipment and the anti-theft steering head lock an optional extra. The US export T120C off-roader had a steel sump guard fitted beneath the engine.

Fuel Supply and Carburettors

Black fuel lines were replaced by transparent plastic and, for the first time, the UK Bonneville was offered with a 'pancake' air filter as an optional extra.

Front Forks and Steering

The new top yoke was drilled to accept rubber-bushed handlebar clamps and the handlebar diameter was reduced from 1in to the current industry standard of $\frac{7}{8}$in. The alteration was made by using shims in the metalastic top yoke clamps so that the owners could revert to the old-style bars if they so desired. Twin throttle cables were used instead of the earlier splitter box arrangement. The controls and fixings were adapted to fit the smaller handlebar diameter and black plastic Amal handlebar grips replaced the 'Triumph' embossed rubber items. The ignition cut-out/kill button was dispensed with.

Electrics and Speedometer

A Lucas 6V alternator fed a MLZ9E 12amp/h 6V battery through a silicone rectifier. Charging was monitored by a 2AR ammeter mounted in the chromed headlamp shell with the new charging circuit protected by a 25A fuse. Ignition was by twin Lucas MA6 coils mounted on the frame's lower tank rail beneath the fuel tank. A Lucas 4CA twin-contact breaker unit with a 12 degree auto-advance mechanism was driven by the exhaust camshaft and mounted in the timing cover.

The ignition system featured an emergency-start facility for use in case of a flat battery. Lucas 88SA light and ignition switches were installed on the left beneath the nose of the hinged dual seat. The dipswitch and horn push was integral, with a quick-action twist grip. The Smith's 140mph Chronometric speedometer, calibrated for 1,600 cable rpm, was made a standard fitment. A Lucas 546 stop and tail light was fitted with the stop light function controlled by a plunger switch mounted on the outer face of the chainguard. A Lucas 8H 6V horn was mounted on a welded bracket in front of the battery. An exhaust camshaft drive was provided for the optional tachometer, with a cable drive take-off point ready mounted on the timing cover.

Rear Suspension

A stiffer rear swinging arm and uprated Girling shock absorbers, with springs calibrated to 145lb/in for the UK and 100lb/in for the US, were fitted.

Seat

Now hinged to the frame at the left-hand side, the new seat retained the appearance of its earlier, bolted-on, counterpart. The seat was given a grey top, white piping around the top edge, black sides and a lower grey rim trim at the bottom. The US West Coast export model had a safety strap fitted to comply with local legislation.

Wheels, Tyres and Brakes

A 3.25 × 18in front wheel with 8in diameter single-leading-shoe front drum brake was mounted in a full-width cast iron hub. The 3.50 × 18in rear wheel was provided with a 7in cast iron drum integral with the 46-tooth sprocket. Fully floating brake shoes were fitted front and back.

US Specifications/Options/Alternatives

High-rise overseas pattern handlebars, including the required additional rubber and cup mounting washers, longer control cables and twin rotor twist grip were specified for the United States. Optional twin 'pancake' airfilters, 3.25×19in front and 4.00 × 18in rear wheels were available for US export.

1962 – THE STATE OF THE INDUSTRY

BSA commissioned McKinsey and Company, a respected US management consultancy, to study the US motorcycle market. This research was based on sales figures supplied by Triumph dealers. In addition, McKinsey and Company was requested to research BSA and Triumph factory production philosophy and to identify possible economies. Predictably the report recommended integration of the companies. However, BSA Chairman Eric Turner was selective about applying the report's results. He disregarded the unpalatable sales projections, instead asking the company accountants to make the projections.

Edward Turner retired as Chief Executive of BSA Automotive Division but retained his directorship on the BSA board. Although Bert Hopwood had hoped for the Chief Executive role on the BSA board, the job went to Harry Sturgeon, ex-Managing Director of the Churchill Grinding Machine Company, a BSA subsidiary.

Triumph practice and policy was now completely under the control of parent group BSA. Sturgeon implemented McKinsey's recommendations and rationalized BSA/Triumph motorcycle production.

Hopwood and Hele were recognized as a brilliant combination but Trident efforts continued to be thwarted by retro-minded Triumph management.

Denis McCormack retired from TriCor after 14 years as president. He was replaced by the company's financial manager, Earl Miller, as Vice President and General Manager. Harry Sturgeon became TriCor company president and toured the United States with Edward Turner in autumn 1964.

Bill Johnson, long-time friend of Edward

The US West Coast version of the 1964 T120R; the 'R' signifies road spec.

Turner and owner of Triumph distributors Johnson Motors, Pasadena, California, died. His financial manager, Wilbur Ceder, took over the running of the business.

Triumph sold 6,300 bikes in the United States. Triumph's US-export models had become ever more diverse and, predictably, in those days of 'Export or Die' economics, production for the US took precedence over supplies for the UK home market.

As the 1960s girl group the Shangri Las might have put it, the Bonneville was now regarded as the undisputed 'leader of the pack', but continual development would be essential to maintain that position.

T120 Bonneville 1964

Price: £320 8s 0d
Commencing engine number DU5825
Models: T120 Bonneville 120, T120C Competition Sports Bonneville T120, T120R Speedmaster and T120C TT Special

Engine

Following the previous year's rearrangement of the nine cylinder head bolts, larger valves were fitted. Inlet valves were increased to $1\frac{19}{32}$in and the exhaust to $1\frac{7}{16}$in. Piston crowns were machined to accommodate the larger valve heads. Amal $1\frac{1}{8}$in. diameter choke 389 Monobloc carburettors were bolted to $1\frac{1}{8}$in inlet port adaptors which were connected by an induction balance pipe to help

650 c.c. TRIUMPH THUNDERBIRD (6T)

The rear semi-enclosure and continued use of the nacelle emphasized the tourer status of the 1964 Thunderbird. The style contrasted starkly with the out-and-out sporting character of the 1964 Bonneville which, five years into its production run, was catering for a clearly defined market sector all of its own.

smooth slow-speed running. The inner face of the crankcase was re-profiled to improve oil scavenge capacity and a larger sump filter screen and revised drain plug were fitted.

Transmission and Gearing
The UK and US T120R roadster continued with a 19-tooth gearbox output sprocket, but the American T120C and the newly introduced T120C TT (US East Coast) Special competition model ran lower gearing through an 18-tooth output sprocket. The US West Coast version of the new T120C TT model ran even lower gearing via a 17-tooth sprocket. A kick-start spindle oil seal was fitted in the gearbox outer cover and, to ease manufacture, wider sleeve gear splines were used within the unit construction gearbox.

Frame
To increase ground clearance and allow the rear brake rod to be routed inside the left suspension unit, the footrests were fitted directly onto the rear engine plates.

Front Forks and Steering
The lower spring carrier was fitted with double-lipped oil seals. The friction steering damper had an inner rubber bush to prevent slackening.

Cycle Parts and Fittings

The front mudguard centre brace was modified to enable one size to accommodate the different diameter wheels used across the range. Apart from the US competition model's polished alloy blades, by 1964 the front guards had reverted to painted steel and from that year were secured by a tubular centre brace and forward stay running over the top of the mudguard. The brace and stay were fixed to new brackets at the top of the fork sliders. Using different plates at this fixing allowed the same mudguard and stays to be adjusted to suit the different types of wheels fitted to the various Bonneville production specifications.

The oil tank, now finished in black, was equipped with a drain plug and an additional lower support. From the oil tank froth tower a large-bore breather tube ran back along the right-hand side of the rear mudguard. The same petrol tank as used in the previous year served on the updated 1964 model, but with striking new stylized divisions lined in black between the gold and 'Alaskan white' colours of that year.

Electrics and Speedometer

A new pull-type stoplight switch was fitted on a deeper section chainguard. For the American market the off-road T120C had a Lucas S55 cut-out switch on the handlebars. Across the range, Smith's magnetic tachometer and 125mph speedometer replaced the earlier Chronometric instruments. Both the rev counter and speedometer were rubber mounted.

US Specification Alternatives

The T120C TT Special claimed a compression ratio of 12 to 1, although in fact it was only 11.2 to 1. However, it really did have $1\frac{3}{16}$in. Amal Monoblocs although these were mounted on $1\frac{3}{16}$ in adaptors that tapered down to $1\frac{1}{8}$in at the cylinder head inlet ducts. This specification resulted in an output of 54bhp at 6,500rpm.

Performance Parts

The list of performance parts available was the same as for 1963.

T120 Thruxton Bonneville

In May 1965, a very special competition bike was made available to the public (albeit a carefully selected public) to satisfy the homologation requirements of Production Class racing. Similar small batches of factory-prepared production racing machines had been built and entered through dealers' racing teams in previous years, but this machine was officially listed in the Triumph catalogue as the T120 Thruxton Bonneville.

However, plans to build fifty of these bikes were frustrated by a crime which still remains

---

Thruxton, the Circuit

The name 'Thruxton' was derived from a venue near Andover, Hampshire, where throughout the 1950s and 1960s, an annual production motorcycle race was held. Covering 500 miles around Thruxton airfield's perimeter track, this race was seen as the most prestigious event of its type. Originally known as the Thruxton Nine Hour marathon, mileage rather than duration later became the crucial factor and the name was changed accordingly. Like other production races, regulations for the Thruxton 500 Mile ensured that competing machines were prepared and equipped as they would be when sold to the public. Only limited alterations from standard specification were allowed, and only then in the interests of safety. No rider could be expected to stay in the saddle non-stop for the full nine hours or 500 miles of the Thruxton, so each competing machine was shared by two riders taking turn about, the change-over coinciding with fuel stops if things went to plan.

In 1965, to the dismay of Triumph's publicity department, as Triumph released the limited edition Thruxton Bonneville to an eager but strictly limited market, the organizers of the Thruxton event made the untimely decision to switch the race venue to the Castle Combe circuit in Wiltshire.

Thruxton Bonneville. The muscular front hub of this example rippling with stopping power provided by a four-leading-shoe brake.

unsolved. The alleged theft of a cylinder head and twin carburettors intended for engine number DU 23156 meant that only forty-nine Thruxton Bonnevilles, one less than planned, reached the end of the assembly line. Thruxton ownership was to remain an even greater privilege than the factory had intended.

Special Features of the Thruxton Bonneville

Although Thruxton Bonnevilles were listed as production machines, the degree of works preparation took them well away from the standard, run of the mill, street Bonnie. An ordinary enthusiast approaching a Triumph dealer for any of the components that formed the crucial elements of the Thruxton package was going to be sadly dis-

appointed. Even when those components were identified in Triumph's 'high performance alternative parts' list, their supply was carefully restricted by the factory. Meriden did not intend that any of the fifty-six Thruxton homologation specials produced by the factory during 1965 and 1966 would be replicated.

Most potent of the Thruxton's modifications was the use of touring profile E 4220 camshafts with larger, 3in radius, cam followers. This camshaft-cam follower combination had the beneficial effect of increasing both valve lift and the duration of opening. The downside was increased wear of the camshaft lobes, a significant problem for the Bonneville even before this performance modification increased the loading on the cam face. To reduce this effect, the Thruxton led the way to positive lubrication of the exhaust cam, with an external small-bore pipe carrying oil from the timing chest to the exhaust camshaft. The rest of the Bonneville range would not benefit from camshaft lubrication until the following year.

To achieve maximum engine efficiency in operation, components were 'Blueprinted' prior to assembly; parts were selected from components with tighter and complementary engineering tolerances. This allowed Thruxton engine parts to be carefully matched with regard to a closer, more efficient, assembly fit and balance. Carburettors reverted to the chopped $1\frac{1}{8}$in Amal Monoblocs with the centrally mounted remote float chamber last seen in 1960. The bikes long upswept exhausts attached to the rear subframe's seat loop by flat metal straps were a ready recognition feature, but more importantly the tapered 'straight through' silencers contributed significantly to the Thruxton's 54bhp output. The standard Bonnie achieved only 47bhp. Those 54bhp

were normally delivered through a standard transmission, but rumours persist that a small number of Thruxtons were discreetly equipped with close ratio gear clusters.

To meet production racing regulations the handlebars had to be clamped in the standard, yoke top mounts; consequently low, 'Thruxton bend' bars were used to provide an acceptable racing posture. Larger 19in wheels front and rear, an 8in front brake cooled by a forward-facing air scoop and a steeper steering head angle with a revised head lug casting all contributed to the Thruxton's improved handling. The familiar parcel grid and tank badges were removed in the interest of safety and weight reduction. Only modest transfers were left to distinguish the rare T120 Thruxton Bonneville as one of Triumph's most sought after motorcycles.

The T120 Bonneville Thruxton; another competition special, this time tailored for UK production racing.

1965 – THE STATE OF THE INDUSTRY

The prototype Triumph 750cc triple was tested in a Bonneville frame. BSA chief Harry Sturgeon saw the 750cc triple as the BSA group's response to the looming Japanese big bike threat.

Kawasaki became the first Japanese manufacturer to open a US distribution office. A total of 609,000 two wheelers were imported by US motorcycle dealers. 33,406 came from the UK, 465,000 from Japan.

After a substantial improvement in production, total Triumph output fluctuated between 600 and 800 bikes per week, with 80 per cent of the machines earmarked for US export. A total of 49 Bonneville Thruxton production racers were made in May.

The Honda CB 450, the 'Black Hawk' 450cc, appeared in direct competition with Triumph twins. The Honda had an electric starter and, thanks to the horizontally-split crankcase, was oil tight.

Velocette introduced the 500cc Thruxton, its last model.

In the United States, Harley-Davidson became a public company. Johnson Motors Inc. imported 6,531 Triumph motorcycles, and TriCor imported 8,807. Since 1958 Triumph had exported 54,400 motorcycles to the USA with a total value in excess of £3.5m. In hopes of improving things still further BSA purchased a controlling interest in Johnson Motors and consolidated the US sales operation with TriCor. A heavy downside was encountered when company executives were asked to sell the BSA models alongside the Triumph range. Dealers who had previously sold either BSA or Triumph were instructed to sell both, which was resented by many dealers.

T120 Bonneville 1965

Price: £362 13s 3d
Commencing engine number DU13375
Models: T120 Bonneville 120, T120C Competition Sports, T120R Speedmaster and T120C TT Special

Engine

The crankshaft's lateral alignment was no longer fixed by the timing pinion bearing against the timing-side right-hand main bearing. Instead, the engine drive sprocket was altered to butt up against the inner spool of the drive side main bearing, so shifting the fixed end of the crankshaft to the left-hand drive side. Anticipated benefits were better primary-drive chain alignment and a more controlled loading of the drive-side main bearing. However the change lasted for one year only and by 1966, although the 1965-style engine sprocket was retained, the lateral location of the crankshaft had been shifted back to the timing side. This was achieved by the reintroduction of the E3300 clamping washer between crankshaft timing pinion and the inner spool of the timing-side main bearing.

As an aid to maintenance a feature intended to establish and lock the engine in its Top Dead Centre (TDC) position was introduced. A threaded hole, normally sealed by a blanking plug, was positioned behind the cylinder block to the right of the crankcase joint. To establish TDC during servicing the blanking plug would be removed from the hole and replaced with a threaded sleeve. A pin was inserted through this sleeve and, as the flywheel was slowly rotated, it was allowed to drop into a slot cut into the periphery of the flywheel at the TDC position. In practice, more significance was attached to a point 38 degrees before TDC, the engine's fully advanced firing position. After a series of changes this 38 degrees before TDC (BTDC) position became the timing reference point marked by the slot.

Minor modifications were made to other engine details. To reduce oil leaks the pressure relief valve was modified and the oil pressure indicator feature was no longer provided.

The $1\frac{1}{2}$in exhaust downpipes received welded tab fixings to allow the installation of an additional exhaust bracing piece across the front of the engine.

From engine number DU22682, aluminium exhaust stubs replaced the original mild steel stubs in the cylinder head exhaust ports. It was

1965 Bonneville T120C TT Special. Manufactured between 1963 and 1967 this was an out-and-out, no frills, competition bike aimed squarely at the American market. The open exhaust pipes tucked in tightly beneath the frame were an especially favoured feature.

hoped that the more compatible coefficient of heat expansion would prevent loosening of the stub in the alloy exhaust port. Sadly, the change only worsened the situation. The softer aluminium stubs collapsed as soon as the exhaust pipe clamps were tightened and so lost their grip on the exhaust port even before the heat of battle was encountered. At engine number DU39464 the steel stubs were quietly reintroduced.

Transmission and Gearing
Armstrong cork friction linings for the clutch were introduced under the original T1362 part number. Additional protection from possible damage by the primary chain was provided for the alternator cable by a longer cable nut. A thrust washer and shorter kick-start pinion sleeve on the main shaft were used to prevent burring and the resultant snagging of the kick-start on the return stroke.

Frame
Only detail changes were made to the frame. The prop-stand lug angle was altered to provide increased stability when parked and the swinging arm bolt was made to fit from the more easily accessed right-hand side. An altered rear brake pedal allowed the brake rod to be operated from the inside of the engine plate to give a straighter pull on the brake cam lever.

The 650cc Bonneville of Ken Buckmaster.

Front Forks and Steering

New forks offering an extra inch of travel and longer, softer, springs were protected by improved rubber gaiters.

Cycle Parts and Fittings

Thicker stick-on rubber knee pads were applied to the fuel tanks of road-going models.

Fuel Supply

An optional extra air filter which fed both carburettors through a replaceable filter element was made available.

Wheels, Tyres and Brakes

The rear wheel hubs featured a new grease-retaining disc and felt washer on wheel bearing. The optional Quickly Detachable wheel was no longer fitted with a taper roller bearing. Instead ball journal bearings were used. The front wheel spindle was changed to suit the new forks.

US Specification Alternatives

A more upright ride position was provided by new high-style overseas pattern handlebars. The mudguards were painted steel for East Coast US and polished alloy for the West Coast.

For 1965 silencers, or mufflers, were produced in a shorter, more streamlined, style. The T120C TT had upward 45 degree folding footrests to comply with US competition regulations.

Performance Parts
The list of performance parts available was the same as for 1963.

1966 – THE STATE OF THE INDUSTRY

To maintain its position as market leader the Bonneville entered a period of rapid change. Rather than wait for the start of the new season to introduce changes in specification, technical updates were incorporated at the earliest possible opportunity. Practicality took precedence over production-line protocol. To add to this sense of urgency in the factory, increased demand from the United States dictated that a growing proportion of Bonneville production was allocated for export.

The 1966 Triumph brochure urged potential customers to 'go modern, go Triumph' and promised 'up to the minute performance'.

Detroit Triumph dealer Bob Leppan used his streamliner 'Gyronaut X1', powered by two 650cc Triumph engines to set a new US record at 245.66mph (395.27km/h). However, his achievement was denied FIM recognition as the total capacity of the paired-up twin-cylinder engines exceeded the FIM's 1,000cc limit.

American Buddy Elmore won the Daytona 200 on a works-prepared 500cc Triumph Tiger 100.

Managing Director Harry Sturgeon died after having restored company moral in the face of the Japanese threat. He was replaced by Lionel Jofeh from Sperry Gyroscope, another motorcycle industry outsider.

The Ogle Design consultancy was commissioned to develop a radical new style for Triumph's 750cc triples. Edward Turner worked independently on the design of a large four-cylinder engine, but it was destined never to be built.

Bonneville Speedmaster 650 cc / O.H.V. / Twin Carburetor / Twin Cylinder

What's new in TRIUMPH '66?

plenty!

It's not easy to improve on a champion. But Triumph for '66 has done it with such new features as more horsepower, higher compression ratio, stainless steel fenders, new race-proven frame, better braking, even new colors. And that's not all. Discover *all* the great new features at your Triumph motorcycle dealer now!

Over 600 Dealers Coast-to-Coast

Western Distributor: Johnson Motors, Inc., P.O. Box 457, Pasadena, California 91102
Eastern Distributor: Triumph Corporation, Towson, Baltimore, Maryland 21204

US-specification stainless steel mudguards and a polished alloy stop and tail light, new features for Triumph in 1966.

Panther motorcycles closed. Francis–Barnett and James motorcycles ceased production as Associated Motor Cycles (AMC) collapsed. AMC was later restructured after a take-over by

go
modern
go
TRIUMPH

WITH UP TO THE MINUTE PERFORMANCE

For 1966 'go modern, go Triumph' with the new look Triumph's 'up to the minute performance'.

Manganese Bronze Holdings. In the new company, Norton was given priority over AJS and Matchless, and both companies followed Panther, Francis-Barnett and James Motorcycles into closure. All Norton single-cylinder models were dropped.

In 1966, a total of seven Thruxton Bonneville production racers were manufactured.

Bonneville T120 1966

Engine

The principal change for 1966 was a new crankshaft and flywheel assembly. By shaving the sides of the flywheel into a stepped profile, $2\frac{1}{2}$lb of dead weight was removed without compromising the 85 per cent balance factor. This reduction produced a quicker throttle response without any increase in engine vibration. To hold things together, longer flywheel retaining bolts were used and a heavy-duty single-lipped E2879 roller bearing was installed on the drive side. Crankshaft lateral alignment location was restored to the timing side by the reintroduction of clamping washer E3300 between the timing pinion and timing-side main bearing.

Following the example set by the specialist Thruxton Bonneville in the previous year, the T120's exhaust cams now benefited from positive-feed lubrication. Instead of the external feed pipe used on the Thruxton, oilways were drilled in the timing-side crankcase to enable lubricant to pass at engine pressure through a metering dowel into drillings in the cylinder block casting and then to the exhaust cam follower tappet guide. At engine number DU42399 a dowel was incorporated in the crankcase/cylinder block flange joint to prevent any loss of oil pressure should the cylinder base joint loosen in service. At the same time $1\frac{1}{8}$in radius R type high-performance sports cam followers became a standard fitment with the E4819 inlet cam and $1\frac{1}{8}$in radius oil-fed cam followers on the E4855 profile exhaust cam. Sealing of the revised push rod tubes was improved by silicone rubber 'O' rings. New oil-fed exhaust and inlet tappet guide blocks compatible with the revised push rod

1966 649cc T120 Bonneville (UK and general export variant)

Price: £349 7s 1d
Commencing engine number DU24875
Models: T120 Bonneville 120, T120R Bonneville
Road Sports, T120TT Bonneville TT Special

Unit construction engine and gearbox.
Red Spot inner and outer valve springs.
12V electrics.

Engine

Cylinder bore	71mm
Stroke	82mm
Cylinder capacity	649cc
Compression ratio	9:1
Claimed output	47bhp at 6,700rpm

Carburettors

Type	Amal 389/203 Monoblocs
Choke size	$1\frac{1}{8}$in
Main jet	260
Pilot jet	25
Needle	Type 'D' (second position)
Needle jet	0.106

Fuel tank

Capacity	4 gallons (Imperial)

Gearbox (four speed)

top	4.81:1
3rd	5.76
2nd	8.17
1st	11.81

Electrics

Ignition	Lucas MA12 coil ignition
Charging circuit	Lucas 47162 AC generator charging through 12V Zener diode
Battery	Twin NKZ 9E up to engine number DU32994; thereafter, a single Lucas PUZ5A
Spark plugs	N4 gapped at 0.25

Tyres

Front	3.25 × 18in
Rear	3.50 × 18in

Brakes

Front	8in drum, single leading shoe
Rear	7in drum, single leading shoe

tubes were installed. Compression was stepped up to 9 to 1 and, although they were originally designed to complement the softer 'quiet performance' Dowson ramp cam profile used on the 6T

Thunderbird, Red Spot inner and outer valve springs with bottom valve spring cups were fitted. From engine number DU29738 larger $1\frac{3}{16}$ in carburettors were used.

From engine number DU39464 the soft aluminium exhaust pipe adaptors were replaced by the original steel type. The electrical system was converted to 12V, but the crankshaft-mounted AC generator and Lucas 4CA contact breaker continued. Some US East Coast export models were fitted with individual chromed pancake air filters instead of the larger black-painted single unit that served both carburettors. Benefits included improved access to the ignition switch mounted on the side panel.

Transmission and Gearing

The layshaft speedometer drive pinion and the speedometer cable take-off on the inner cover of the gearbox were deleted. To help rationalize speedometer calibration for the various combinations of gearbox and final-drive ratios, speedometer drive was now taken from the rear wheel. The increased compression ratio resulted in a longer kick-start being fitted for extra leverage. A larger diameter clutch adjusting screw was fitted in the outer pressure plate after engine number DU31168.

Frame

A new head lug casting with a steering head angle of 62 degrees instead of the previous 65 was introduced. By popular demand, lugs to enable the attachment of a fairing were incorporated. To accommodate wider tyres, the swinging arm was widened to $3\frac{3}{4}$in by moving its right-hand fork by $\frac{1}{4}$in. A new ignition key switch with a more secure Yale-type barrel was fitted to threaded studs welded onto the redesigned battery carrier.

Front Forks and Steering

From engine number DU27672 a modified lower yoke, used with the slimmer 1966 fuel tank, allowed an increased steering lock and tighter turning circle. The white handlebar grips used early in the year later reverted to black. The

Colin Craig's T120 Bonneville can be recognized as a 1966 model despite the many after-market updates. Typical of any true enthusiast's bike, Colin's machine has been modified with a twin-leading-shoe front brake from a 1969 model. To simplify maintenance a single carburettor has also been fitted.

alloy steering damper sleeve was replaced by plastic from DU31119.

Wheels, Tyres and Brakes

The front brake was much improved by a 46 per cent increase in friction area. This was achieved by anchoring the spokes onto an external raised flange on the wheel hub, so increasing the internal area of the drum available for braking and allowing the use of wider brake shoes. The standard (non-QD) rear wheel had a new 7in diameter cast iron rear brake drum with bolt-on sprocket. The drive sprocket of the QD wheel was cast integrally with the brake drum, as previously.

Cycle Parts and Fittings

The fuel tanks were revised. In the UK the parcel grid was retained and the capacity fixed at 4 gallons but the tank was sculpted to a slimmer, more tapered shape.

Stateside, a new $2\frac{1}{2}$ US gallon 'slimline' tank became a US Bonneville icon. This small capacity teardrop-shaped tank proved very popular and further emphasized the Bonneville's sporting image. At the same time as the new tank was fitted, the tank top parcel grid was dropped and new badges introduced. The 'harmonica' grille, used since 1957, was out and the chromed 'eyebrow' badge, featuring the Triumph logo in black on a white background, was in.

A 6-pint oil tank was mounted on two rubber spigots at the top, one below. The oil tank featured an adjustable rear chain oiler metering screw and feed fitted in the filler cap neck.

Various mudguards were specified during the 1966 model year. In the UK, steel versions were painted in 'Alaskan white' with a 'Grenadier' red centre stripe and gold lining. In the US, stainless steel mudguards with rolled edges were favoured for Bonneville roadsters, with the front guard losing the heavy front-wheel stand and receiving instead a slimmer tubular lower stay. UK seats were two-tone grey and black, whilst in the US some roadsters and most off-roaders sported plain black.

Electrics and Speedometer

With the change to a 12V electrical system came new Lucas MA12 ignition coils, still discreetly tucked away under the petrol tank. These 12V coils, the Yale-type ignition switch and a Zener diode to control charging of the paired Lucas MKZ9E batteries were the principal changes to the electrical system for this year. (A single Lucas PUZ5A 12V battery was used after engine number DU32994.) After engine number DU 32898 the Zener diode was fitted to an improved right-angle heat sink due to 'heat soak' problems encountered on US West Coast models. The chromed headlamp shell continued to carry a Lucas 2AR ammeter and, after engine number DU31565, a green ignition warning light and red main beam warning light were fitted. The tachometer was driven by a right-angle cable drive from the end of the exhaust camshaft.

US Specification Alternatives

Stainless steel mudguards were fitted along with a new polished alloy stop and tail light. US road models used straight-through absorption-type mufflers whilst the T120C TT was fitted with 1.75in diameter open racing pipes tucked in beneath the engine and finishing below the swinging arm pivot. In the United States, these pipes proved 'mighty' popular. As a safety feature, an engine cut-out was fitted on the right handlebar.

1967 – The State of the Industry

By 1967 the pace of change was slowing and consolidation of the existing Bonneville design could be considered. The factory resolved to update its range of fastening threads from the old BSF (British Standard Fine), Whitworth and CEI (Cycle Engineers Institute) to UNF and UNC (Unified fine and coarse). This was no mean undertaking, and the change from British Standards meant that tooling costs at Meriden soared. Even though the new threads forced in the introduction of an updated range of components and a completely new parts numbering scheme to go with them, economics dictated that the change be made as quickly as possible.

In 1967, at the age of 66, Edward Turner retired from the BSA board. With the Speed Twin, Turner had conceived and created the modern vertical-twin motorcycle engine, which led the way for motorcycle development for the next three decades. He had recognized the potential of Triumph's American motorcycle market virtually before any United States market could be identified and he had established an industry and distribution network to serve it. The product, manufacturing base and dealer network had all benefited directly from his perception and foresight.

Demand from the American market could not be supplied quickly enough. Even though 60 per cent of Meriden production was allocated for US export, Harry Holland, Export Manager at Meriden later admitted 'It was never possible to ship Johnson Motors or Triumph Corporation quantities sufficient to fully satisfy either' (Quote from Ivor Davies *Triumph – The Complete Story* (Crowood MotoClassics).)

John Hartle won the Isle of Man Tourist Trophy on a Bonneville.

BSA took over production of Triumph's sales catalogue. 28,700 Triumphs were sold in the United States. The UK national speed limit was raised to 70mph (113km/h) and the breathalyser drink/drive deterrent was introduced.

Royal Enfield sold off production machinery and stock, Matchless ceased production and Ariel motorcycles closed.

Umberslade Hall

Umberslade Hall, the 'no expense spared' research and development facility common to BSA and Triumph operations was set up under Lionel Jofeh, BSA group Managing Director. With its 300 staff and £1.5m per annum operational costs, the facility soon became known amongst Meriden staff as 'Slumberglade Hall' or 'Marmalade Hall'. The top management of BSA Automotive Division were increasingly being recruited from outside the industry. Few staff at the research centre had motorcycle industry backgrounds and many came straight from university. A large computer system had been installed but had not been tamed. Umberslade's principal contribution to the Bonneville was the controversial 1971 P39 'oil in frame' chassis. Both the BSA and Triumph 650cc twins suffered from the ill-considered introduction of this frame.

T120 Bonneville 1967

Price: £355 0s 10d
Commencing engine number DU44394
Models: T120 Bonneville 120, T120R Bonneville Road Sports, T120TT Bonneville TT Special

Engine

Initially, in the early months of 1967, Amal Monobloc type 389/95 carburettors were fitted. Later, after engine number DU59320, Amal Concentric type 930 carburettors with a metric choke size of 30mm were used. To improve idling, the inlet port adaptors were connected by a rubber balance pipe. New Hepworth and Grandage 'Hepolite' pistons were fitted in place of the Meriden manufactured items and, from engine number DU47006, heavy-duty RR56 polished alloy connecting rods with a thicker cross section were installed.

To prevent the 'wet sumping' condition (that is, the motor running with an excess of engine oil left in the crankcase) that sometimes occurred after long, fast, stretches, a new oil pump with increased scavenge chamber capacity was introduced.

For 1967, the E3134 exhaust camshaft was copper plated and, in the continued endeavour to reduce cam lobe wear, the exhaust cam followers were lubricated through a new metering dowel via a filter gauze at the timing cover bolt. To prevent the possibility of a blockage the metering jet was equipped with a 'jiggle pin'. After engine number DU63043 timed tappets were used to feed lubricant to the cam faces through the cam followers. As the cam follower was lifted off its base circle, a cut-out in the cam follower stem aligned with an oilway port in the tappet block. This allowed a pressurized supply of oil onto the cam face immediately before the initial cam lift. As the follower fell back, the cut-out moved out of alignment and the oil supply ceased. The tappet block was fitted with an 'O' ring base seal after engine number DU63241.

From engine number DU51771, a random spark condition, experienced after the change to 12volt electrics, was cured by the introduction of a 160 degree dwell auto-advance unit cam operating the Lucas 4CA contact breakers. Lucas 6CA contact breakers introduced the following year further improved the ignition timing. The exhaust front pipes were given short support straps fixed to the front crankcase mounting bolts instead of the cross brace previously fitted. The black 'big box' air filter was dropped in favour of a return to twin chrome-plated pancake air filters for general export models, although standard UK models were still bereft of air filters any type.

Transmission and Gearing

The layshaft spline corners were radiused to prevent the stress fractures previously experienced in competition use. The clutch nut tab washer was replaced by a locknut with CEI thread pending a later change to UNF (Unified fine) thread. A 'Loctite' plastic gasket was used to prevent oil seeping past the gearbox sprocket. Alternate engagement dogs on the second gear mainshaft pinion were removed after engine number DU 64758, but restored by DU 64858.

Frame

To cater for the various styles of petrol tank fitted to the current range, threaded steering stops were

The 1967 T120R, shown here in US specification with stainless steel fenders and no tank mounted parcel rack.

introduced. An extended headlug to accommodate the location peg of the new steering lock was fitted to the front fork top crown lug. The tank mounting lugs were tapped with UNF threads.

Front Forks and Steering
A new fork top was lug fitted to carry a Yale-type barrel lock, with a peg which located in a hole in the extended headlug flange. The gaiters were secured by spring clips, not worm drive straps. An 'O' ring oil seal was included in the dust excluder sleeve nuts to stop seepage along threads.

Fuel Tank, Cycle Parts and Fittings
The mudguards were steel, painted in 'aubergine' with an 'Alaskan white' centre stripe and lined in

gold. The petrol tank was-two tone with an 'aubergine' top half and 'Alaskan white' lower section divided by gold lining. There was a black finish to the frame oil tank and switch panel. In the United States, stainless steel mudguards were fitted.

Seat
A grey cross-quilted top with black sides, white piping and grey lower rim trim was provided. The seat's new profile featured a slight step half-way along which carried the pillion passenger slightly higher than the rider. Additionally, the rear end of the seat was ramped upward to assist passenger retention under hard acceleration. The Triumph logo was emblazoned in gold across the rear panel. Although the plan had been to equip all

Detail shots of sectioned T120 650cc engine; this example carries the Amal Concentric carburettors first fitted in 1967.

road-going models with this seat and fit off-roaders with an all-black version, most US machines were equipped with black seats whether intended for off-road use or not.

Electrics, Instruments, Speedometer
The Lucas stator coils were now in an encapsulated unit within the primary chaincase. A more powerful Lucas 6H horn was fitted under the front of the petrol tank. There was a new 150mph grey-faced Smith's speedometer (1,600 cable rpm) and tachometer. A Stat-O-Seal washer was used to seal the tachometer drive against the crankcase and prevent the drive from working loose.

Wheels, Tyres and Brakes
Home and general export models had a 19in front wheel of Triumph design with a 3.0 × 19in Dunlop ribbed tyre. The front brake was an 8in single leading shoe in a full-width cast iron hub.

The 18in rear wheel carried a 3.50 × 18in Dunlop Universal K70 Gold seal tyre. The rear brake was a 7in cast iron drum integral with chain sprocket. Both the front and rear brakes had fully floating shoes.

US Specification Alternatives
1967 was the end of the road for the TT Special. Although plans for a 1968 version had been made, the T120C TT Special was phased out of

Triumph's US catalogue at the end of the season. Other US-specification Bonnevilles were fitted with straight-through absorption-type mufflers.

1968 – THE STATE OF THE INDUSTRY

1968 was the high point of Bonneville production and a vintage year for the bike. The 1968 sales catalogue boasted of 'Precision, Power and Performance' before going on to claim the Bonneville as 'surely the most potent, fully equipped road machine in standard production today'.

Noise and emission legislation began to bite on the performance produced by all road-going bikes.

In October 1968 Honda announced its four-cylinder, single overhead camshaft CB750 at the Tokyo Motorcycle Show. Later in the year, at the Honda America annual sales convention in the Sahara Hotel, Las Vegas, US dealers were given a dramatic introduction to the new multi-cylinder Honda when it was ridden up to the first floor of the hotel and into their reception room.

T120 Bonneville 1968

Price: £355 0s 10d
Commencing engine number DU 66246
Models: T120 Bonneville 120, T120R Bonneville Road Sports

Engine

Improved Hepolite pistons with reinforced crowns were fitted to counter combustion chamber overheating problems. Green Spot outer valve springs were specified to give an increased loading characteristic when the valves were fully open without any change of loading in the closed position. The rocker arm oilway feed via the ball pins was deleted after engine number DU78400. This allowed an improved flow of lubricant to reach the exhaust cam. A secondary benefit from this change was realized after engine number DU

79965; the rocker arm oilway was no longer drilled and consequently the finished rocker arm was left stronger.

Even though many enthusiasts saw the old Amal Monobloc as a better carburettor, 30mm Concentrics continued to be fitted. Minor modifications were made to cure a sticky carburettor slide problem encountered the previous year. Air filters were made standard for UK later in the 1968 season and the standard filters already fitted to US-export models were made to screw directly onto the carburettor intakes.

Cylinder barrel location was improved by the introduction of twelve cylinder block/crankcase fixing studs and, at long last, enough clearance was provided in the barrel fining to enable the proper torque to be applied to the nuts. The first 1,800 machines produced during 1968 were equipped with one of three variations on the timing location theme. Initially, Top Dead Centre (TDC) was used as the reference, with the locating hole on the upper face of main crankcase casting behind the cylinder barrels. After engine number DU 66246, the locating hole was moved to the front of the crankcase below the engine mounts and the flywheel slot repositioned accordingly. This 'improvement' made the locating hole harder to access and prompted a further change. Ultimately, from engine number DU 74052, the location bung was placed in its original position behind the cylinder barrel with the corresponding slot cut into the flywheel at the 38 degrees before Top Dead Centre (BTDC) position.

Further assistance with ignition timing came with the provision of a stroboscopic timing disc accessed through the primary-drive cover. This allowed the timing to be adjusted using service tool D2014: a stroboscope timing plate. Two lines scribed on the rotor enabled stroboscopic setting of the timing without the need for an external timing disc. After engine number DU83021, a permanent fixed pointer was fitted which, when aligned with the 38 degree BTDC mark on the rotor, showed the ignition fully advanced timing position.

1968 T120 Bonneville 650cc featuring the full width front hub with twin-leading-shoe brake and pancake air filters. On this example the tank top parcel grid is not fitted; it was officially deleted from the 1969 specification to improve safety.

New Lucas 6CA contact breakers with independently adjustable points were fitted and a deeper timing cover provided to protect them from the elements. To save space on the new contact breaker backplate, the capacitors were moved to a new location beneath the fuel tank's front mounting. After engine number DU82146, wear on the nylon heels of the contact breakers was reduced by the provision of felt oil pads which lubricated the cam. The timing of each cylinder could at last be set individually and without compromise.

Transmission and Gearing

A new clutch shock absorber spider was secured by a UNF self-locking nut requiring the use of a UNF threaded extractor D652/3. Externally, the most prominent change was the provision of an inspection cover over the alternator rotor which enabled the timing to be adjusted using service tool D2014, the strobe timing plate.

The gearbox mainshaft was lengthened to allow use of UNF threads at both ends. The kick-start mechanism received UNF threads, the layshaft speedometer drive was deleted and a new mainshaft high gear with extended nose was provided. This bore directly against the oil seal, and in turn required a new inner cover plate to the primary-drive case. A revised camplate plunger gave a better gear change action.

Frame

Few changes were made to the frame during 1968. Heavy-gauge tubing was tried on the front frame between engine numbers DU75430 and 75449 and the steering lug socket was altered to prevent any chance of the peg still being engaged as the bike was ridden off. The propstand was remodelled with a curved end instead of its original 'foot' and the propstand mounting lug on the frame modified to suit. The rear subframe was modified by the addition of spigot pegs carrying the left-hand side panel. After the relocation of ignition and light switches this left side panel served as a toolbox cover but it remained inadequately held at the top forward flange by a threaded plastic knob. The later addition of a locking spring did little to increase security and loss of both cover and toolkit continued to be all too frequent.

Rear Suspension

From engine number DU81196 the swinging arm was manufactured from heavier 12 standard wire gauge (swg) tubing instead of the previous 14swg tube. This tougher tubing, stronger corner fillets and a new swinging arm mounting lug gave the rear end significantly increased rigidity. Additionally, to aid greasing of the spindle, a breather hole was drilled in the cover plate.

Front Forks and Steering

New forks with two-way 'shuttle valve' oil damping looked virtually identical in appearance to the previous forks but provided much improved performance. Initially, from engine number DU68636, the fork assembly continued to be manufactured with CEI form threads. Only later were Unified threads used on stanchions, bearings and cap nuts.

Cycle Parts and Fittings

The fuel tank was now secured with three rubber-mounted studs and nut fixings. Thicker knee grips were fixed to the fuel tank's sides with adhesive instead of the previous screw fixings. 'Stat-O-Seal' washers were used to help align the petrol tap without compromising the seal at the fuel tank boss.

Seat

The quilted top seat gained extra padding and pressed hinges were used instead of the previous forged type. The UK finish remained two-tone grey with black sides and white piping, but a chromed plastic rim trim was added along the bottom edge. For the US market the same seat was finished in black with a black plastic trim. From engine number DU75452, the West Coast seat strap was superseded by the fitting of a chromed grab rail at the rear of the seat. This rail also became a standard feature of the East Coast model from engine number DU77018.

Electrics, Instruments, Speedometer

The ignition switch was now sited on the left-hand headlamp bracket and the three-position lighting switch fitted into the headlamp shell. As in the previous year, the 150mph grey-faced Smith's speedometer and tachometer were used. The Zener diode was mounted on a 'finned egg' heat sink in a cooler location beneath the headlamp.

Wheels, Tyres and Brakes

A new twin-leading-shoe front brake was installed in the existing full-width 8in front hub. With its functional mesh-covered air scoop and external linkage controlling twin brake cams, the new brake made efficient use of the self-servo effect produced at the leading edge of each brake shoe, doubling the braking potential derived from the self-servo of the previous single-leading-shoe brake.

Reservations were voiced over the security of the front brake cable in the brake plate anchor point. From engine number DU70083 the outer cable was drilled and pinned into position to prevent it pulling out of the anchor point if the front brake were to be run out of adjustment.

Although the brake had a characteristically spongy feel due to the more complicated operating linkage, it was nevertheless effective in use and consequently well received by the bike-buying public.

The rear brake remained the 7in cast iron drum with bolt-on 46-tooth sprocket on the standard wheel and 7in cast iron drum with integral sprocket on the Quickly Detachable (QD) option. Both brakes had fully floating shoes.

Wheels were 3.00 × 19in at the front with a ribbed tyre and 3.50 × 18in with Dunlop K70 Gold Seal Universal on the rear.

US Specifications/Options/ Alternatives

For the US, the bike was given a 2.5 US gallon fuel tank with amber side reflectors fitted under the front mounts. The gearbox sprocket carried 19 teeth.

Wheels for the US West Coast were 3.25 × 19in at the front with a ribbed tyre and 4.00 × 18in with Dunlop K70 Universal at the rear. The East Coast model was equipped with a 3.50 × 19in front wheel and ribbed tyre and 4.00 × 18in rear. US-specification wiring was modified to allow the headlamp to be used only when the ignition was switched on. Straight-through absorption-type mufflers were fitted.

Performance Parts

The list of optional performance parts was fast dwindling as they became normal features of the standard model.

1969 – THE STATE OF THE INDUSTRY

1969 saw the peak of the Bonnies' racing success. The Thruxton 500 mile marathon event was won at an all-time record speed by a Triumph Bonneville, with other Bonnies following in second, fifth, sixth and seventh places. The 1969 success marked the end of the Bonneville's consecutive run of Thruxton wins which had started in 1965.

Malcolm Uphill won the Isle of Man Production TT on a Bonneville at an average speed of 99.99mph (160.88km/h). During the race Uphill achieved the event's first lap of over 100mph on a production motorcycle; completing the circuit at an average speed of 100.37mph (161.50km/h). Other Bonnevilles claimed third, fifth and sixth positions.

A Triumph Bonneville ridden by Malcolm Uphill and co-rider Steve Jolly secured a class win in the Barcelona 24-hour endurance race. The Swedish Grand Prix was also won by a Bonneville.

Triumph's publicity slogan for the UK was 'Top line for '69', and in the US 'Leave it all behind on a Triumph '69'; many managers in British motorcycle manufacturing would have liked to do exactly that.

The UNF thread conversion programme was completed on the engine and gearbox components. The cam wear problem was finally laid to rest thanks to the use of tougher nitrided camshafts. The Bonneville benefited from more power and a softer exhaust note due to the fitting of an exhaust balance pipe. Manufacture of the gearbox shaft and gears shared with the Trident was moved to Small Heath but complications arose over the components' dimensions. Parallel production of components differing only fractionally in size forced a complete parts re-numbering scheme.

Meriden was producing 900 bikes per week, but quality control suffered badly. The resulting warranty costs showed significant rises over the equivalent year-on-year figures for the previous decade.

All US distributors were assimilated into one company: the Birmingham Small Arms Company Incorporated (BSAC). BSACI was headed by Peter Thornton from the company's headquarters in Verona, New Jersey. Thornton had come to BSACI from a position as an advertising agency executive engaged on the Triumph account. In his new role as company chief, Thornton divided BSACI into three subsidiaries: Triumph Motorcycles Incorporated; BSA Motorcycles Incorporated; and Top Gear, a motorcycle accessory supplier.

Donald Brown of BSA Inc. (New Jersey) consulted Illinois-based designer Carl Vetter regarding a re-styling project for the BSA triple. The new model was intended to appeal to the American taste for chopper-type bikes.

In Germany, BMW released a radically revised new line up of modern motorcycles, and as a

Chief tester and works road racer Percy Tait takes a break whilst testing a travel-stained Triumph T120 Bonneville.

Percy Tait takes a turn around the Meriden traffic island as he follows his regular test route on a unit construction Bonneville in the 1960s.

result BMW sales figures increased dramatically. The Honda CB750 was given a warm welcome by customers when the first machines reached the US showrooms in June of 1969. Honda's radical new four-cylinder machine marked a step change in the competition faced by Triumph.

In total 32,721 British bikes were exported to the USA during 1969, most of them manufactured by Triumph. During the year, Honda America sold over 30,000 examples of the CB750 alone, Kawasaki introduced the H1 500cc triple and Suzuki further developed the two-stroke GT 750. The Bonneville's marketplace was already crowded and the squeeze was increasing.

T120 Bonneville 1969

Price: £373 19s 9d
Commencing engine number DU85904 to DU 90282 and JC 00101 onwards
Models: T120 Bonneville 120, T120R Bonneville T120R

Engine

The introduction of nitride-hardened camshafts at last put an end to the cam wear problem so long suffered by the Bonneville. Replacement nitrided camshafts were also made available for retro-fitting to earlier bikes. To avoid any confusion a capital 'N' for nitride was stamped on each shaft so treated. UNF threads were applied to the crankcase halves, gearbox inner and outer covers,

Dave Lewis bought his 1969 T120 new from a Cheshire dealership, the only letdown being the pre-delivery preparation. After being properly set up by Hughie Hancox at the Meriden factory the bike was transformed and has delivered reliable service ever since. The direction indicators are one of Dave's after-market additions.

and to the timing and primary-drive covers. The capacity of the oil pump was again increased, this time on the supply side. A larger diameter feed plunger was fitted into a new oil pump body and, from engine number DU88714, the crankcase residual oil level was increased by lifting the scavenge pipe by $\frac{5}{8}$in. An electric oil pressure sensor fitted on the timing cover controlled an oil pressure warning light mounted on the headlamp shell.

A change to Unified thread on the tachometer drive gearbox provided scope to switch the fixing to a left-hand thread, thus preventing the continual loosening of the drive when in use.

From engine number DU85904, updated Hepolite pistons were fitted. These had a thicker domed crown and a shorter, heavier cross section, gudgeon pin. New connecting rods were introduced at engine number GC23016 and the opportunity was taken to use con rod bolts and self-locking nuts with UNF threads. The finer ramp angle of the new Unified threads meant that the tightening torque for the big-end bolts was reduced from 28lb.ft to 22lb.ft. The Amal 930 Concentric carburettor's pilot jet was replaced by a fixed calibrated drilling and the main jet swapped from 210 to 190. The needle jet was changed from 0.107 to 0.106.

Home and general export variant of the 1969 T120 Bonneville. The operating mechanism of the front brake allowed an improved routing of the brake cable and the tank-mounted parcel rack was no longer specified.

Principally as an aid to manufacture, the cylinder head stud holes were press fitted with steel sleeves in order to provide an additional safeguard against damage when machining and polishing the inlet ports.

New castellated push rod tubes were introduced at the start of the season to stop, or at least slow, the loss of oil from the 'O' ring end seals. The new tubes relied upon 'Viton' 'O' ring seals. At the top end these bore against the cylinder head push rod tube counterbore, and at the bottom they maintained a diametral oil-tight fit over the tappet guide blocks. However they did not work and, from engine number PD 32574, an additional silicon rubber seal was mounted in a sleeve press fitted to the lower end of the push rod tube, although this provided only a marginal improvement. The castellations at the top of the push tube provided location in the cylinder head counterbore without presenting a barrier

to oil draining down the tube back to the crank-case.

Manufacture of the 1969 model was already in progress by October 1968 when a new heavier fly-wheel was combined with the existing crankshaft. The effect was to produce a smoother delivery of torque and to mute the more resonant engine vibrations. The engine's overall balance factor remained unchanged.

Security was becoming a prime consideration and in 1969 Triumph responded to increased pressure from international police authorities to help combat crime. From engine number DU 86965, crankcases had a raised pad indented with multiple Triumph logos over which the official engine number was stamped. Any attempt to alter the engine number would result in the pattern being defaced, thus making illicit changes more difficult.

The exhaust system was fitted with a balance

Detail of the 1969 T120 motor equipped with Amal Concentric carburettors and the pancake air filters first specified the previous year. For UK use the filters carried coarse paper elements.

pipe running horizontally between the two down-pipes. First seen on the Thruxton Bonneville production racers in 1965, this pipe enabled the efficient straight-through absorption-type mufflers previously fitted for US export to be made standard UK equipment without any increase in noise.

Transmission and Gearing

Many detail changes to the gearbox were made for 1969. Outwardly, a new kick-start with UNF bolt was fitted whilst on the inside, from engine number DU88630, a new camplate was provided. A new gear change quadrant was fitted at engine number JD26313 and, at the beginning of the season, third gear ratios were shifted from 22/24 to 22/23. The teeth of these new pinions were given an additional finishing process to allow smoother running and were known as 'shaved' gears. From engine number CC15546, main and layshaft diameters were increased with a corresponding change to internal pinion sizes. By the end of the year the internal changes made represented almost a total revision of the gearbox.

Frame and Rear Suspension

No changes were made to the frame for 1969, but the rear swinging arm was made from tougher tubing. The Girling shock absorbers were now supplied without dust covers and displayed chrome-plated springs, emphasizing the sportier 1969 look.

Front Forks and Steering

Forks, now $\frac{1}{4}$in wider thanks to new top and bottom yokes, were able to accommodate a larger section front tyre. From engine number AC 10464, extra $\frac{5}{16}$in holes drilled into the stanchions improved rebound damping control. The steering damper assembly was replaced by a chromed steering stem top nut, although the steering damper could still be specified as an optional extra.

Cycle Parts and Fittings

A new range of fuel tanks was introduced and a new tank badge brought in to go with them. The 1966 to 1969 'eyebrow' style Triumph logo within a winged surround had been usurped by a badge that displayed the similar, although smaller, Triumph motif within a squarer 'picture frame' surround.

Electrics and Speedometer

A new higher output Lucas RM21 encapsulated stator allowed the fitting of dual domed 'wind-tone' horns beneath the front of the fuel tank from engine number DU89530. These powerful horns were mounted on stronger brackets and required relays to cope with the increased current needed to power them. The surfeit of extra power produced by the new stator might well have encouraged the change to the even louder horns which were fitted after engine number CC 14783. A new rear number plate bracket enabled the fitting of the US-style Lucas L679 rear stop and tail light.

The headlamp-mounted oil pressure warning light was wired into the ignition circuit, and would only illuminate if pressure dropped whilst the ignition was turned on.

Seat

The quilted seat cover was made of grey aerated material and the seat base was fitted with threaded mounting holes for the tubular grab rail standard on the rear of US machines.

US Specifications/Options/ Alternatives

A twin rotor twist grip and longer control cables were provided to allow the use of US specification high-rise bars. A 19-tooth gearbox final-drive sprocket provided lower overall ratios.

1970 – THE STATE OF THE INDUSTRY

1970 is recognized by some as the final year of the authentic Bonneville. Even though the ill-conceived changes made to the frame for the 1971 season would later be corrected, there remained a subtle and lasting alteration of the bike's character. Nevertheless the Bonnie was still on a roll.

Malcolm Uphill repeated his win of the production TT, but this time on 'Slippery Sam', his famous race-prepared Trident.

In the US, Triumph Corporation of America (Tricor) made a move into limited motorcycle manufacture on its own account. In 1969, the American Motorcycle Association had introduced an increased 750cc capacity limit for over-head valve engines used in dirt track competition. Although American riders were more than keen to have a Triumph machine that took full advantage of the increased capacity allowance, Meriden was reluctant to produce a 750cc machine for such a restricted market. This left Tricor with customers demanding a machine that was not produced, a position that could not be allowed to continue.

The answer came from good old American resourcefulness and ingenuity. Successful drag racer and accessory manufacturer Hubert 'Sonny' Routt marketed a range of Webcor big-bore kits designed to boost the capacity of Triumph's 650 twin to near AMA's 750cc limit. Tricor recognized that these kits could be a quick-fix solution to its problem and promptly ordered over 200, specifying that they be carefully packaged and finished to look like genuine Meriden products.

The kits comprised of new iron barrels, rings, circlips, gudgeon pins, head gaskets, cylinder base flange gaskets, tappet feed plug and a centre head bolt complete with washer. In other words, all that was needed to lift capacity to 750cc. Also included were 0.008in oversize forged pistons to fit the 3in cylinder bores.

The kits were fitted to standard T120R machines before they were uncrated. A 'T' suffix was stamped into the crankcase after the Meriden model coding on the engine number, but the frame numbers of the modified bikes remained unaltered. The 'T' suffix and a small 'MC' (for Motor Castings, the foundry commissioned for the job by Routt's operation) sited at the base of the cylinder casting near the tappet block were the only outward evidence of the modification. To complete the conversion, dealers were instructed to fit 376/100-200 main jets in the carburettors.

AMA homologation rules specified that at least 200 machines be manufactured for sale. Tricor completed 145 T120RTs and Triumph's West Coast HQ in Duarte, California built another 55. Mystery surrounds the rumoured production of an additional four 750cc machines that were said to have been produced. The venture ended with over 200 happy customers and AMA approval for the T120RT to compete in its events.

Two years later the genuine article, the Meriden-built 744cc T140 Bonneville, appeared.

T120 Bonneville 1970

Price: £420 5s 3d
Commencing engine number JD24849
Models: T120 Bonneville 120, T120R
Bonneville T120R

Engine

New nitrided camshafts and new camshaft nuts with UNF threads, but now without the slotted breather disc, were fitted. Instead of the timed engine breather operated by the induction camshaft, crankcase ventilation was provided by three holes drilled in the drive-side crankcase. Positioned behind the main bearing these three holes vented into the primary chaincase, which itself was vented to atmosphere via a right-angle elbow pipe behind the clutch and a breather pipe clipped to the left side of the rear mudguard. In addition to its welcome simplicity, this new breather system had the additional merit of maintaining a constant level of lubricant in the primary chaincase; any surplus oil was able to drain back into the crankcase via the three breather holes.

The timing gears now had tapped holes enabling the use of gear pullers for easy removal. The engine sprocket spacer previously deleted was restored. The float bowls of the Amal 930 Concentric carbs were equipped with plastic drain plugs.

Transmission and Gearing

From engine number AD37473, the gearbox inner cover was modified to allow use of a shorter selector rod and heavier gauge main bearing circlip. After engine number ED51080, aluminium bronze selector forks with integral rollers replaced the original steel selector fork and, after ED50244, a precision pressed camplate and indexing leaf spring were introduced. Each modification represented an improvement but, inevitably, each contributed towards a more complicated reassembly procedure.

Other minor transmission modifications included rerouting of the alternator cable to emerge from the inner face of the primary-drive chaincase above the gearbox and, as part of the new crankcase/primary drive ventilation system, a breather cover behind the clutch which was fitted to act as a lubricant retaining baffle at the external breather elbow.

Frame and Rear Suspension
A new adjustable-stop prop stand was introduced. New triangular front engine plates mounting onto cross tubes welded into the front downtubes of the frame helped to speed initial factory assembly and subsequent engine removal. Girling rear suspension units now featured improved castellated load adjuster sleeves which were more resistant to water and grit.

Front Forks and Steering
There were minor changes only to the front forks and steering: internal oil bleed holes were introduced in the stanchions, from engine number AC 10464; and new mudguard mounting lugs were provided. The hard chromium plate applied to the outer surface of the stanchions represented a significant improvement.

Seat, Cycle Parts and Fittings
The fuel tank received new colours: 'astral red' with silver background and gold lining.

The capacity of the oil tank, now painted black to match the opposite side panel, was increased to $5\frac{1}{2}$ pints (equivalent to 6 US pints).

Electrics and Speedometer
Smaller oil-filled Lucas 17M 12 ignition coils were now fitted beneath the fuel tank. From engine number ED44339, new, larger, windtone horns received an additional sliding bracket that allowed improved clearance between the horns and front mudguards when the front forks were fully compressed. The old headlamp was fitted with a modified bulb holder, a minimal change that nevertheless merited a new part number.

Wheels, Tyres and Brakes
The same 3.50 × 18in rear wheel now had UNF threads on the rear hub, brake drum, sprocket bolts and speedometer drive. No change was made to the brakes apart from a flat steel strip rear brake anchor plate which replaced the previous tubular pattern.

US Specification Alternatives
The US-specification bike claimed 52bhp at 6,500 rpm.

A twin rotor twist grip and longer control cables were provided to accommodate high-rise bars and a 19-tooth gearbox sprocket provided lower overall gear ratios.

The wheels were 3.25 × 19in Dunlop K70 Universal on the front and 4.00 × 18in Dunlop K70 Universal on the rear. The fuel tank carried $2\frac{1}{2}$ US gallons. US bikes were finished in the same colours as UK models but their fuel tanks featured a swept wing styling panel, finished in silver with gold lining.

1971 – THE STATE OF THE INDUSTRY

In 1979 the BSA group lost £8.5m. This was to be the last year of production for most of the BSA range. Lord Shawcross became chairman of the group, at the suggestion of Department of Trade and Industry, and Eric Turner and Lionel Jofeh retired. The BSA Group was nominally 'sold' for £1 to Manganese Bronze Holdings, already owners of Norton, AJS Matchless, Villiers, Francis Barnett, James, and Velocette.

Velocette went into liquidation.

For the 1971 season, a new frame developed by Umberslade Hall, the Research and Development Department at the BSA Group Engineering Centre, was to provide the foundation for both the BSA 650cc twin and the Bonneville. The efforts of Triumph's own Development Department at Meriden were focused on developing the three-cylinder Trident for racing. Under the supervision of Bert Hopwood and Doug Hele, Triumph achieved significant success in the 1970 and 1971 race calendars. Far-sighted suggestions that Daytona-style race-replica road bikes form part of a future model range were briefly considered but not followed up.

On the Bonneville production line, a short

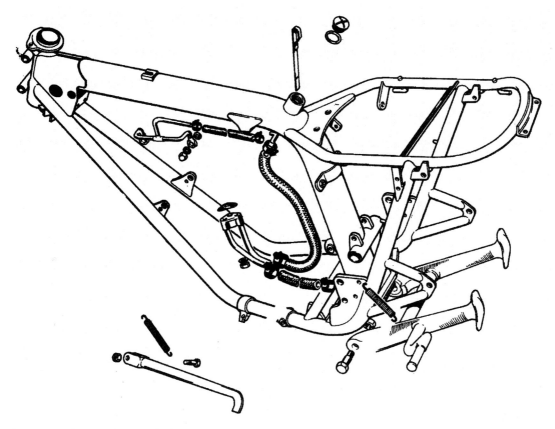

The controversial 1971 'oil in top tube' frame. Designed at the Umberslade research facility, the new chassis was viewed with dismay by production line staff

delay was anticipated before drawings for the controversial 'oil in frame' P39 chassis design would arrive from Umberslade Hall. Workers at the Meriden factory occupied their time by producing the annual quota of Tiger 100s ahead of schedule. Then, as Tiger 100 parts ran out, Bonneville and Trophy engine and gearbox units were assembled, tested and stored away ready for installation in the new and eagerly expected frame. By October still no drawings for the Bonneville chassis had been produced and the staff reverted to playing chess. Imaginative use was made of leftover engine components. Oil pumps ranked as pawns, rockers served as rooks and valve springs doubled as queens on packing case chess boards as the 'Big Wait' dragged on.

On 25 November interest flared when the Group Managing Director summoned staff to a meeting in the works canteen. Once there, they heard nothing of any material shortages or delays due to design difficulties with the new frame; only that the year's wage increases would be dependent upon improved productivity. Puzzled staff and would-be workers returned thoughtfully to their chess sets.

When at last the drawings for the P39 frame did arrive an initial example was quickly assembled and a fundamental flaw revealed. It was found that the Bonneville motor would not fit; to install the engine/gearbox unit in the frame, production staff were required to remove the rocker boxes assembly. Only later, when the engine was mounted in the frame, was it discovered that the rocker box could not be refitted in situ.

Only after eighteen modifications, each one a compromise of long-established production-line practice, were Meriden staff able to squeeze the engine into the frame, reassemble the top end, and restart Bonneville production. Not until Christmas 1970, over three months behind schedule, could manufacture of the 1971-specification Bonneville start. Conspiracy theorists amongst the staff at the Meriden factory were convinced that the BSA parent group intended that the 1971 Bonnie should not have survived; subsequent developments suggested that they may have had a point.

T120 Bonneville 1971

Engine

A series of revisions to the cylinder head and rocker box assembly were required before the engine could be fitted into the controversial 1971 frame. After the rocker box had been internally milled to give the increased internal clearance required to allow assembly, four locating dowels and four two-section head bolts were used to secure the rocker box to the cylinder head.

However, not all engine modification resulted from the changed chassis. A new flywheel was secured by updated bolts and washers to the 1963-style crankshaft. The push rod tubes lost their castellations, instead each had three holes at the top end for oil drainage, and at the bottom the 1969-type silicon washer and pressed-on sleeve continued. On the timing-side crankcase, a new one-piece oil pressure relief valve was secured by a UNF thread that was conveniently compatible with earlier crankcases. At the base of the frame's main tube oil tank a sump plate with a fixed 'top hat' screen filter and sump plug was fitted. Later models had a separate plate and filter to ease servicing.

The crankcase breather arrangement introduced in the previous year had rendered the drive-side crankshaft oil seal redundant and it was consequently deleted. Bearings were in short

---

1971 649cc T120 Bonneville (UK and general export version)

Price: £558
Commencing engine number NE 01436
Models: T120 Bonneville 120, T120R Bonneville T120R

A new cylinder head was adopted to allow completion of engine top end assembly after the unit had been fitted into the frame. The 'oil in top tube' chassis prompted many detailed changes in specification and in assembly procedures.

Engine

Cylinder bore	71mm
Stroke	82mm
Cylinder capacity	649cc
Compression ratio	9:1
Output	47bhp at 6,700rpm

Carburettors

Type	Amal Concentric
Choke size	30mm
Main jet	180
Pilot jet	20
Needle	Type 'Std' (first position)
Needle jet	0.106

Fuel tank

Capacity	4 gallons (Imperial)

Gearbox (four speed T120)

Top	4.95:1
3rd	6.15
2nd	8.36
1st	12.10

Electrics

Ignition	Lucas 17M 12V oil-filled coils
Charging circuit	Lucas 47205 alternator
Battery	Lucas 12V PUZ5A
Spark plugs	N3 gapped at 0.25

Tyres

Front	3.25 × 19in
Rear	4.00 × 18in

Brakes

Front	8in alloy hub drum, twin leading shoe
Rear	7in alloy hub drum, single leading shoe

Independently designed by Edward Turner after his retirement, this 349cc DOHC twin would have been marketed as the BSA Fury and the Triumph Bandit. Although listed for the 1971 season it did not go into production owing to the company's financial problems.

supply during 1971 so, from engine number GE 27029, as an expedient measure, the timing-side crankcase, shaft journal and timing pinion were modified to take a more readily available metric-sized ball bearing. As part of the updated look for 1971 the exhaust was revised with new down-pipes and full-length tapered megaphone silencers clearly specified to accompany the new frame and restyled side panels.

Transmission and Gearing

From April 1971 the Quaife five-speed gearbox conversion originally available as an after-market addition was offered as an option. Bikes with the five-speed box carried the 'V' suffix in their designation, for example T120RV. The five-speed internals had been previously used by the factory's race team and could be fitted into the current gearbox casing without alteration. Minor modification also enabled the five-speed box to be fitted to earlier machines.

Late in the 1971 season the clutch centre shock absorber was strengthened. The bolt-on rear wheel sprocket now carried 47 teeth resulting in lower overall gearing and the need for a 106-link rear chain.

Frame and Rear Suspension

A completely new one-piece duplex (twin front downtube) frame presented what many felt to be an excessive seat height of 34in (0.85m). Of welded construction and with its 3in diameter main tube spine doubling as a 4 pint oil tank for the engine lubricant, the new chassis was received with mixed feelings, especially by shorter riders. Although engine vibrations were more pronounced, possibly due to the more rigid duplex construction, the new bike was comfortable and nobody could deny it steered well. The new rear suspension units were fitted with chromed springs rated at 110lb.

1971 T120R 650cc Bonneville. The principal change was the completely new duplex frame. The 3in diameter top tube of the one-piece welded chassis carried 4 pints of engine lubricant but the ride height was seen as excessive by many riders.

The late-1971 T120R Bonneville for the home and general export markets. A revised specification introduced late in the season combined US-style high-rise bars and megaphone silencers with the UK 4 (Imp) gallon slabsided 'breadbin' type fuel tank.

Front Forks and Steering

Entirely new forks were carried on adjustable taper roller steering head bearings. In the style of Italian Ceriani units, the 1971 forks had aluminium sliders which were controlled by a new internal damper tube and valve assembly. The internal springs gave 6in of suspension travel but early fork seal failures demanded the fitting of revised seals later in the year. The stanchion tubes went without rubber gaiters and the chrome plated wire headlamp brackets were rubber mounted onto top and bottom steering yokes. At the bottom of the sliders the front wheel spindle was clamped by aluminium end caps, each secured by four studs. The optional steering damper was still available by request.

Seat, Cycle Parts and Fittings

Along with the new black-painted 'oil in top tube' frame came an updated 3 gallon (Imperial) fuel tank. Rubber mounted and secured by a single BSA-style central fixing bolt, the new tank retained traditional Triumph curves and the 'picture frame' tank badges but had new chrome styling strips. The rubber knee pads were discontinued. Later in the year a flat-sided 'breadbin' 4 gallon tank sporting Triumph decals on each side was fitted for UK and general export.

Mudguards were being worn shorter that season; at the front, wire mudguard stays were clamped in threaded bosses on the fork sliders and a combined grab rail and stay supported the rear guard. Later in the year an extra centre stay was added to the front mudguard. For the home and general export market the mudguard carried a black plastic number plate. The 1971-season tanks and mudguards were finished in 'Tiger gold' with a black centre stripe lined in white. Finished in black aerated vinyl with black piping and ridges running across the top, the new seat had an external lockable catch and was hinged on the right, thus opening in the opposite direction to previous models. The Triumph logo was emblazoned in gold on the back panel. To fit the new frame the seat was shorter and no longer had the split-level feature. Beneath the seat the new ventilated side panels housed two easily accessed air filters connected to the carburettors by rubber pipes.

Electrics and Speedometer

Flashing indicators were introduced and new Lucas switchgear collars on each handlebar coped with the increased control functions. The switch cluster on the left handlebar operated the horn, the dipswitch and the headlamp flasher, whilst the indicator switch and ignition cut-out were housed on the right. The indicator lamps had amber lenses mounted on chromium bodies secured by hollow stems. At the front the stem passed through the bent-wire headlamp bracket and was bolted inside the headlamp shell. The rear turn indicators and a new Lucas L679 stop and tail light were carried on a new rear number plate bracket mounted on the back mudguard. The flat-backed 'pan' shaped headlamp shell carried a two-position rotary light switch and three warning lights, red for oil and ignition, green for main beam and amber for direction indicators. No ammeter was provided and the previous dual 'windtone' horns were replaced by a forward-facing Lucas 6H horn fitted beneath the fuel tank.

The matching 150mph speedometer and tachometer were protected by rubber cups and mounted on twin brackets clamped under the chromed cap nuts of each fork stanchion.

Wheels, Tyres and Brakes

Both front and rear wheels were built on new conical alloy hubs and carried Dunlop K70 Universal tyres. The front rim was fitted with a 3.25 × 19in tyre and the rear with a 4.00 × 18in tyre.

The 8in twin-leading-shoes front brake fitted for 1971 featured bigger brake shoes, a large forward-facing air scoop and two exit vents. In spite of these features, the stopping power was down on the previous TLS brake. This was possibly due to the shorter operating arms which turned the brake cams in opposite directions and could all too easily slip out of adjustment. A later addition to the operating mechanism was a spring threaded over the inner cable between the two operating arms. This maintained tension on the cable as the brake was released and was intended to prevent the cable dropping out of location if poorly adjusted. The front brake was adjustable through an access hole in the alloy hub, which was normally sealed with a rubber bung.

In April 1971, the 7in rear brake received a longer upward pointing operating arm, thicker fulcrum pads and thicker liners. A new, more effective, return spring was introduced with the longer brake operating arm. The rear wheel no longer benefited from the useful Quickly Detachable option and the rear brake no longer had fully floating shoes. Both front and rear drum brakes had steel friction liners pressed into the alloy hubs.

US Specification Alternatives

The US specification included a twin rotor twist grip and longer control cables to accommodate the high-rise bars. A 19-tooth gearbox sprocket provided lower overall ratios. US-regulation mufflers were also fitted.

1972 – THE STATE OF THE INDUSTRY

BSA group losses were reduced to £3.3m. The company decided on severe staff reductions which reduced the workforce from 3,000 to a total of 1,000, staffing two of the company's three factories. It was secretly planned that 1,750 redundancies would be made at Meriden. To achieve these economies, the group's motorcycle manufacturing operation would have to be consolidated at two production sites yet to be chosen. Most Triumph workers already suspected that Meriden would not be one of the chosen two.

The Umberslade Hall research centre was closed in January 1972.

A total of 250,000 Bonnevilles had been built. Eric Turner formally resigned as chairman but retained an advisory position. Denis McCormack resigned from TriCor. The Carl Vetters triple was launched carrying a Triumph badge due to the poor financial state of BSA.

The few Bonneville riders who claimed to be suffering from altitude sickness might have been exaggerating but, just the same, rapid remedial action was applied to the previous year's seat height problem. Modifications to frame, front forks, rear suspension and the seat itself were implemented to bring the height down to a more manageable 32in (0.8m). Although the factory maintained that the seat was no higher than the original Bonneville's at $31\frac{1}{2}$in, many still felt that the 1972 Bonnie was more than a fraction higher.

As a provisional measure to help shift earlier stocks already assembled in the previous year's taller frame, the front forks were shortened and the seat width reduced. To lose a last half inch, even the padded upholstery of the seat was made thinner. The resulting Spartan steed developed a distinct forward tilt that did not help the handling. Additionally, due to the bike's forward inclination, the fuel tank's full capacity was not available for use because the rear-mounted petrol taps were sited too high for the tank to drain completely.

T120 Bonneville 1972

Price: £569 (or with the five-speed gearbox option, £629)
Commencing engine number HG30870
Models: T120R Bonneville 120R, T120RV Bonneville 120RV

Engine

New big end bearing caps were fitted and, after engine number CG50464, the old-style two-section oil pressure relief valve was reintroduced. Wider section timing pinions with threaded holes for the fixing of gear pullers were used later in the season. A new cylinder head was introduced at engine number XG42304. The exhaust pipes no longer fitted over steel exhaust stubs but instead were a direct push fit into the exhaust port. The finned exhaust clamps were retained mainly for the sake of appearance although they may have served by providing increased heat dissipation. Other features on this new head casting were the flanged inlet port adaptors

For the US market the 1972 T120RV Bonneville was offered with the 3 US gallon 'round' fuel tank finished in 'tiger gold' with a new style of 'cold white' tank flash and horizontal lower panel.

which bolted onto threaded studs instead of screwing directly into the inlet duct.

Completely new rocker boxes incorporated two flat finned inspection covers instead of the four old-style rocker caps. Four modified internal cylinder head bolts and associated rocker box bolts were used to secure the revised rocker boxes and help hold down the cylinder head casting.

Transmission and Gearing
The clutch operating mechanism was improved.

Frame and Rear Suspension
At engine number CG 50414 the Umberslade 'oil in top tube' frame was modified. The integral rear subframe was re-engineered and shorter Girling rear suspension units used to reduce the overall height of the frame.

Front Forks and Steering
The aluminium outer fork sliders no longer had a polished finish. A new stem and bottom yoke assembly was secured by a 24UNF threaded top nut.

Seat, Cycle Parts and Fittings
The side panels and air filter boxes were reduced in height to correspond with the changed dimensions of the second series 'oil in top tube' frame. The slabsided 'breadbin' 4 gallon petrol tank with stick-on knee grips was standard fitment for the UK and general export models. In the United States, the 'breadbin' 4 gallon tank was available as an option; conversely traditionalist UK customers could order the US-style round tank. The seat was made narrower and with less padding to minimize height ASL.

Electrics and Speedometer

After engine number CG50414, a new ignition coil mounting provided greater component accessibility. By popular demand the functions of the handlebar switches were reversed; indicators, engine cut-out and headlamp flasher were positioned on the left and the dipswitch and horn were moved to the right. A louder Lucas 6H horn was fitted and the flasher indicators supported by shorter stems. The speedometer and rev counter continued unchanged.

US Specifications/Options/ Alternatives

For the US, the five-speed box was standard on the T120. US-specification mufflers were provided and an alternative paint styling was available on the tank.

8 Industrial Turmoil

1973 – THE STATE OF THE INDUSTRY

In August 1973, at the age of 72, Edward Turner, designer of the 1937 Speed Twin, died at his home in Dorking.

In an effort to save the British motorcycle industry, on 17 July 1973 a company was formed which combined the resources of Norton Villiers and BSA/Triumph The new company, Norton Villiers Triumph Limited (NVT), was headed by Dennis Poore, chairman of Manganese Bronze and Norton Villiers. NVT equity was held jointly by Manganese Bronze and BSA.

Poore believed that the salvation for the British motorcycle industry lay in the two-factory plan. Neither of the two factories referred to in the plan were Meriden; instead it was proposed that the relatively small motorcycle plant at Meriden be closed and Triumph production consolidated at the old BSA Armoury Road factory in Small Heath, Birmingham. This plant was more than three times larger than Meriden and offered scope for greater efficiency. Nortons would continue to be manufactured at the Wolverhampton factory.

Given that the losses at BSA group were running at £4m per year, this arrangement allowed essential economies to be made, and made undeniable financial sense. NVT had been formed to save money, not to run extra, inefficient, factories. The Department of Trade and Industry had given a conditional commitment to provide £5m in financial support for NVT and there was an obligation to spend it wisely.

Secrecy was maintained over the closure plan. In fact, initial talk of financial support from the DTI at first appeared to underwrite the future of Meriden along with the rest of NVT. However, informed opinion continued to express doubts over the strategy. The support on offer was seen by those critical of the deal as the maximum cash that could be justified in the political climate of the day, but still insufficient to enable the development of a new range of models, which would be essential to an independent, commercially viable future for the British motorcycle industry.

In its issue of 10 June 1973, the *Sunday Times* maintained that the planned re-organization gave the industry no more than the chance to stagger on with its current superannuated model range for another two or three years, and did not provide the claimed lifeline to the new generation of world-beating bikes that was really needed.

At Meriden, the production run for 1974 was to be a brief one. As the factory geared up for the new season, a meeting between management and trades union officials was scheduled for Friday, 14 September 1973. The midday meeting was requested by Meriden shop stewards intent on restoring proper working relations between staff representatives and the new parent company, NVT. Relations had soured after a previous pay-related dispute, and this meeting was meant to be an opportunity to restore them. In blissful ignorance and with a vague sense of optimism, the morning shift commenced production.

By Friday lunch-time, as the pre-planned staff meeting was in session in the works canteen, rumours that the factory was to close begin to circulate amongst the workforce. Initially the whispers were greeted with derision; any coherent closure plan would surely have been enacted before the works holiday in August, not as the

Coventry Evening Telegraph
Friday, September 14, 1973

Night Final

Coventry Evening Telegraph

No 25,536 FRIDAY SEPTEMBER 14 1973 3p

MERIDEN WORKS TO CLOSE

THE Meriden factory of Norton Villiers Triumph — where BSA and Triumph motor cycles are made—is to be closed by February 1 next year.

This shock news came today when Mr. Dennis Poore, the NVT chairman, met staff and workers at the Meriden factory.

The announcement comes less than four months after the BSA-Triumph motor cycle interests and those of Norton Villiers were merged in the new NVT company.

The Meriden factory employs 1,700. Some of them may be absorbed in other NVT plants where motor cycle production is to be concentrated.

By H. G. PRITCHARD, Evening Telegraph Business Editor

Announcing the closure the company said that arrangements were being made for employment to be maintained until next February.

Staff and trade unions had been informed and further discussions would be taking place with their representatives.

The statement went on: "In some cases the opportunity of alternative employment may be available within the group.

"The motor cycle business of the BSA company suffered a loss of some £4 million in the year to July 31, 1973, before any provision for relocation. This result followed losses of approximately £4 million and £8 million in the previous two years, including re-organisation costs.

"In the six weeks of the current year this business, now a section of Norton Villiers Triumph, has suffered further losses approaching £500,000.

Economies

"The maximum business capable of development within available group resources during the next few years can easily be physically contained within the group factories in Birmingham and Wolverhampton, but not, in practical terms, within any combination of two which includes Meriden.

"It is only by economies which this concentration of production will permit that these losses can be eliminated and the foundation laid for a healthy British motor cycle industry.

"Demand for Triumph motor cycles continues at a high level throughout the world. There is every intention to continue and increase manufacture in other group factories where employment is expected soon to rise by at least 1,000 people as output builds up."

Mr. Poore . . . met staff and workers at the factory today.

'We will fight' —shop steward

By JOHN STOLLS

A LEADING shop steward at the Meriden factory gave this warning on hearing the news:—

"The men are going to fight to keep this plant open."

Mr. Philip Green, of the Transport and General Workers' Union said this after talks between shop stewards, union officials and Mr. Leslie Huckfield, M.P. for Nuneaton.

Mr. Green, said the men felt very strongly about cutting off production of machines which the Americans were "mad about."

Production, he said, was 1,400 machines a week earlier this year but it was now down to 500 to 600 weekly.

"We have been starved of components.

"Mr. Poore, the chairman of Manganese-Bronze, had to take Triumphs to get his hands on the more viable part of the B.S.A. group when he bought it.

US regard

"Now he does not want us, he just chucks us to the wall."

Mr. Green said that 30 per cent of the work had been contracted out at a cheaper rate in the last few months.

He and other Triumph workers had seen for themselves in the U.S. how Americans regarded the machines.

"They are mad about Triumphs but if they find out that a Triumph bike had been assembled in America they won't have it. They want the real thing.

"Who is going to make Triumphs better than Triumph? Ninety-five per cent of the British bikes are made here.

"We have just to prove to them that we can produce the bikes.

Mr. Green.

Mr Dennis Johnson, convenor of the Transport and General Workers' Union at the factory, said: "We are absolutely disgusted at this. It is abysmal.

"Mr. Poore has told us that no blame can be laid at the workers' door. But we are even more disgusted to find that the Press knew about this before our members have been told."

Meetings would take place next week following full consultation with all the unions concerned.

Another shop steward was bitter about the closure. "Give us the parts and we

Continued on Page 20

'Complete surprise' for MP

Mr. Keith Speed—the motor cycling MP for Meriden who rides a Triumph machine—was this afternoon "completely surprised" by the news of the closure announcement.

"I was talking to the Motor Cycle Association and Mr. Chris Chataway just a couple of days ago and nothing was said. I'm sure that if they had known, they would have mentioned it in confidence."

Mr. Speed said he always understood that the Triumph and Norton names would be kept independent and that there would be no badge engineering.

"It would be crazy to put a Triumph badge on a Norton and vice versa," he said.

11 pc home loans shock

A SHOCK 1 per cent rise in the building societies' mortgage rate to a record 11 per cent was recommended by society chiefs today—and there could be worse to come.

The increase is coupled to a ¾ per cent rise to 7½ per cent in the rate to investors in a bid to boost the inflow of funds to the societies and prevent an even worse mortgage famine.

The rate changes were announced by the council of the Building Societies' Association after a 2½-hour meeting in London.

New borrowers face the higher rate immediately and it will be up to individual societies to decide when to alter the rate to existing borrowers.

The new investment rate comes in on October 1.

After the meeting, the association's chairman, Mr. Leonard Boyle, said he hoped the present rise would be the last for three or four months, but further increases were not impossible.

The existing 10 per cent rate was fixed only on August 16, when it went up by one-half per cent. Sir Hubert Newton, a chairman of the large Leek and Westbourne Building Society, has predicted it might go as high as 14 per cent.

Bishop at Butlin's

THE Bishop took 400 people down to Butlin's and there, in that most curious of religious settings, planned an evangelistic revival.

Muriel Tibbs went with them to Clacton and today on Page 18, describes "all the fun of the faith."

• Man killed in Coventry Page 4
• Jobless man "victimised" ..... Page 9
• Fire death inquest ... Page 15
• Wood End post move Page 18
• Lord Stoke's denial ... Page 21
• Mayor for Kenilworth! Page 22

Courtaulds win Russian order

Courtaulds in Coventry today announced a £26 million order from Russia for a triacetate synthetic fibre plant.

It will be the seventh that the company has sold to the USSR. Negotiations are said to be at an advanced stage and the contract — currently being drawn up — should be signed within a few weeks.

Linwood stay out —Ryton halted

Evening Telegraph Industrial Staff

ALL AVENGER production at Chrysler's Ryton plant will stop tonight because 6,000 of the company's Linwood men voted today to remain on strike

Today's majority decision to remain out was described by Mr. Peter Griffiths, Chrysler's director of industrial relations, as "effective support for the Coventry electricians who are seeking payment of £250.

"The company cannot, in the current circumstances, pay this without breaking the law."

Mr Griffiths said that the halting of the Ryton lines was another serious blow to the company following the six-week dispute, and "a threat to the company's long-term position."

"Three thousand of Ryton's [illegible]

work as from the end of today's shift, 1,800 will be kept employed "for a few days" next week when the company takes an inventory.

TALKS END IN DEADLOCK

Talks between Chrysler management and the electricians' union at the Department of Employment in London today (See Page 23) ended in deadlock after a four-hour meeting.

It is unlikely that the department will make any further moves towards reconciliation.

LATEST

IN BRIEF

Dearer power in October

INCREASES in electricity tariffs, averaging less than 3 per cent nationally, have been passed by the Price Commission. They take effect early in October.

FIFTEEN pound pay rise for senior journalists on provincial daily and weekly papers in England and Wales was claimed today by the National Union of Journalists. It would give minimum rates of £1675 on small weeklies and £52 on daily papers in larger cities.

SYRIA is to complain to the U.N. Security Council against yesterday's "Israeli aggression" in air battle.

PILOT of an Ethiopian airliner carrying Emperor Selassie set off a hijacking alarm in error, while flying over Italy today but quickly reported all was normal aboard.

MR. HEATH warned today that it would be unthinkable to let wages run riot in Phase Three

LATE STOCKS

War 3½: 31¼; Whitbread "A" 76¼; A.P. Cement 196¼; Glaxo 243; I.C.I. 242; G.E.C. E.K. 146¼; I.C. Holdings 97; Plessey 124; Guest 266¼; Tube Inv 382; ATV "A" 91; Granada "A" 82; Cad Sch-weppes 60; Unigate 67¼; Utd. Biscuits 69; Eagle Star 164¼; Legal & Gen. [illegible]

Beecham 267¼; Brit. Oxygen 84; Dunlop 81; Metal Box 278¼; Reckitt Colman 239¼; Sears "A" 37; Unilever 336¼; Brit. Leyland 34¼; Shell Trans 276; Land Sec. 304; Debenhams 113; GUS "A" 278; Marks 167; Utd. Drapery [illegible]

Bad news travels fast and confirmation of the unthinkable arrived with the late edition of the Coventry Evening Telegraph; closure date for the Meriden factory would be 1 February 1974.

factory returned to work for the 1974 season's production.

Confirmation of the unthinkable arrived with the late edition of the *Coventry Evening Telegraph*; the closure date for the Meriden factory was scheduled to be 1 February 1974. After 15 years, Bonneville production was due to cease.

In immediate response to the closure threat, industrial action was taken and the bold assertion 'the workers say the factory will not close' was issued to the press. NVT's survival plan, outlined at the meeting of 14 September was to be the subject of eighteen months of high-profile political debate and a bitter industrial dispute. Whether or not Meriden was to close, no Bonnevilles or any other bikes would be produced for some time to come.

On the evening of Friday, 14 September 1973, the Meriden site was taken over by the workforce and the factory gates blockaded.

The initial response of the 1,700 employees to the news of the planned closure had been bewilderment. Later, when staff heard the reasons for the closure decision, bewilderment turned to anger. After successfully fighting for over three years to meet production targets in the face of what they saw as inept management, material shortages and Umberslade's chaotic design decisions, staff moral collapsed into bitterness when they read in the next day's papers that Dennis Poore saw: '. . . the Meriden factory as having consistently fallen short of requirements, not because of any action of the workpeople, but because management had been unable to organize an adequate flow of supplies.'

Their bitterness was compounded when reminded in the same day's papers (*Coventry Evening Telegraph*, 15 September 1973) that Christopher Chataway, a major player in the setting up of NVT and the minister responsible for industrial development at the DTI, had made Meriden's survival a condition for the Government's support for the agreement.

Dennis Johnson, convener for the Transport and General Workers Union, told of a shared sense of betrayal over the closure and voiced concern that staff heard of the decision only after the newspapers had been told. Resentment amongst the workforce rapidly grew into a determination to prevent closure by direct action.

On Monday, 17 September 1973, Leslie Huckfield (Labour MP for Nuneaton), Keith Speed (Conservative MP for Meriden) and Maurice Edelman (Labour MP for Coventry North) held a meeting with Christopher Chataway at his London office. Already newspaper reports were speculating on the possible sale of the Meriden site and its value. The three MPs were reminded that the placing of £4.9m of taxpayer's money with NVT was seen as an investment by the Government, not a grant. Although no dividends were expected for three years, a return in the shape of a competitive British motorcycle industry was the DTI's ultimate aim.

T120 and T140V Bonneville 1973

Price: £434.53 (T120 649cc) or £625.34 (T140V 744cc, five speed)
Commencing engine number JH15366 (650 cc) and JH15435 (750cc)
Models: T120R Bonneville Road Sports, T120RV Bonneville five speed, T140V Bonneville five speed, T140RV Bonneville five speed

Engine

Technically, production of the T120 continued largely unchanged through 1973. From engine number JH15345 the 724cc T140V was introduced with a bore/stroke ratio of 75 × 82mm. The gradual application of UNF threads continued and at this point in the programme the T140 found itself with four outer cylinder head bolts having CEI threads and four inner bolts wearing UNF. At engine number XH22019, the introduction of a new cylinder block casting with Unified threads enabled the bore to be increased to 76mm producing the Bonneville's ultimate capacity of 744cc. This new cylinder block was shorter and allowed the engine to be installed in the frame with the rocker boxes intact. Shorter push rods and push rod tubes were specified to suit the new block dimensions.

The home market 1973 750cc T140V Bonneville, with five-speed gearbox, front disc brake and chromed mudguards front and rear.

At engine number CH29520, a new cylinder head was fitted and two $\frac{5}{16}$in central head fixing bolts used to help secure it. Along with the introduction of this 10-bolt head came an increase in the oilway diameters, new valve guides and a flat bar head steady fixed to the central rocker box studs. In the crankcase a new crank shaft was attached to the old-type flywheel with improved bolts and ran on a heavier duty metric timing-side main bearing. This revised crankshaft/flywheel combination produced a balance factor of 74 per cent. Hepolite pistons with three-part oil control rings and reinforced crowns were attached to strengthened con rods by thicker gudgeon pins. The crankcase castings were updated to cope with the increased power and greater vibration stresses produced by the bigger engine. Main bearing bosses were substantially thickened and the block/crankcase joint altered to accept the wider cylinder bores.

The 30mm choke Amal type 930 Concentric carburettor continued to be fitted, but now with a 210 main jet. New cast aluminium $1\frac{1}{8}$in inlet port adaptors, a new inlet manifold balance pipe, new valve guides and bottom valve spring cups were specified along with a combination of hot inlet and milder exhaust cam profiles intended to limit vibration. Although the 744cc engine did not develop its full potential torque due to the apparently inappropriate mix of cam profiles, both rider and bike were able to enjoy a smoother ride.

Later in the season, at engine number AH 22965, a longer silencer with a rounded reverse cone end was briefly introduced only to be superseded by a straight-sided reverse cone silencer of still greater length. This silencer was the final version and was fitted until the end of production at Meriden.

Transmission and Gearing

To transmit the 750's increased power, a $\frac{3}{8}$in pitch triplex primary-drive chain was used with an appropriate engine shaft drive sprocket and

So popular was the light and responsive Bonneville engine that many specials were built using the motor fitted into a variety of frames. The most attractive specials of the period were built around Rickman's Metisse frame kit.

The finished results had a lean and purposeful look whether intended for road . . .

. . . or track use.

clutch drum. An improved clutch centre shock absorber was installed and the clutch springs re-rated to carry the increased torque. The new high gear assembly and the high gear pinion were located by a circlip instead of the previous pressed-on shoulder location. The new triplex primary drive was also incorporated on the T120. The T140 was fitted with five-speed transmission as standard and a 20-tooth gearbox sprocket was used to suit the altered ratios.

Sadly, the T140V's five-speed gearbox was prone to jump out of gear, usually at the most inopportune moments. The cure proved to be a conversion kit that amounted to almost a complete revision of the gearbox internals. Introduced midway through the 1973 season, the kit provided replacement mainshaft first and second gears, layshaft first, second and third gears, layshaft first gear selector fork and the layshaft first gear driving dog. Another midseason addition was the T150 Trident gearchange operating camplate and indexing plunger.

Frame and Rear Suspension
A dipstick was attached to the oil filler cap on the top tube tank and the fairing lugs were deleted from the steering head. The rear suspension units were shortened to help reduce overall height.

Front Forks and Steering
Mudguard mounts on front fork sliders were made stronger. The 1973 Bonneville benefited by having the T150 fork legs clamped by new top and bottom yokes with provision for the hydraulic brake master cylinder. The tops of the stanchions were protected by metal shrouds which featured rubber-mounted headlamp brackets and carried the ignition switch on the left. For the UK, rubber gaiters protected the forks from the elements; the US versions went without.

Seat, Cycle Parts and Fittings
The 1973-season seat continued with the transverse ribs in the aerated top panel upholstery, the all-black finish and the gold Triumph logo on the rear panel. New features were a slight lift towards

One of the many after-market modifications available to the Bonneville owner, a primary drive kit utilizing a toothed rubber belt. Claimed benefits were longer life and quieter, maintenance-free, running.

fork slider acted upon a 10in diameter chrome-plated cast iron disc fitted to the two-piece alloy hub. The brake's fluid reservoir was mounted on the handlebar in unit with the master cylinder and brake lever assembly. Performance was a big improvement on the conical hub twin-leading-shoe brake of the previous year but rapid pad wear developed if, as often happened, the disc lost its chromium plate finish.

On the rear brake a revised brake cam and underslung operating arm were fitted midseason.

US Specification Alternative

Standard tank for US was the 2.5 gallon (US measure) 'Slimline' version. The US compression ratio was 8.6:1, UK 7.9:1. The US version was given 8in high-rise bars while the UK spec had the flatter traditional style. The US-specification rear tyre was upped to 4.25 × 18in.

the rear of the seat, a courser grain in the material used for the side panels and a bright chrome trim around the bottom edge. The earlier Triumph-type catch and locating plunger replaced the previous year's seat latch and the hinges were restored to the left-hand side.

For all models except the T120, the front and rear mudguards were made longer and chromium plated. The T120 continued with the limited protection offered by the previous year's shorter painted mudguard blades.

Fuel tanks for both the 650 and 750 models remained the same, but the 750 was again given the upper hand by having exclusive access to the new season's colours: 'hi-fi vermilion' and gold. Due to the extensive use of polished aluminium and chromium plating on the T140, the fuel tank became the only area in need of paint. Consequently, market-driven variations of colour could be produced without need to co-ordinate the finish of the associated mudguard or side panels.

Wheels, Tyres and Brakes

The prime feature for 1973 was a new disc brake. A single piston caliper bolted to the left-hand

1974 – The State of the Industry

At the Meriden factory the production run for 1974 had been short and none too sweet.

Dennis Johnson, convenor for the Transport and General Workers Union spoke for those barricaded inside the Meriden factory when, in October 1973 he claimed: 'It's our factory, and we are not going to let it go without a fight. All we want is a practical solution other than closure.' By the end of 1973 the possibility of a workers co-operative buying and running the factory themselves was being seriously considered.

The last machine assembled prior to the formation of the Meriden Workers Co-operative was NJ60083, a 1974-specification model manufactured in October 1973.

The general election of 28 February 1974 brought a Labour Government and hopes of a more sympathetic hearing for those inside the gates of Meriden.

In March, desperate to secure its factory and the stock of over 2,500 completed and 1,500 unfinished motorcycles, with a total value in excess of £2m, NVT sought to issue a writ. Tony Benn, in his capacity as Secretary of State

Dennis Johnson, convenor for the Transport and General Workers Union, spoke for those barricaded inside the Meriden factory when in October 1973 he claimed 'It's our factory, and we are not going to let it go without a fight. All we want is a practical solution other than closure.'

for Industry after the Labour election victory, intervened by declaring his support for the workers and negotiating a token release of goods from Meriden. As a Government Minister and Britain's longest serving MP, Benn could not be seen to condone the Meriden workers in an illegal act. Given that in legal terms the 'work-in' amounted to nothing more than an act of mass trespass, the Secretary of State for Industry was treading on thin ice. He agreed to provide consultants to work with convenor Dennis Johnson and the other Meriden shop stewards on a viability study into the workers co-operative proposal. If the study proved favourable, additional help to prepare a case supporting the project was to be made available. Business failures were rife in Britain and Benn saw public

ownership and Government financial support as a form of State-supplied 'first aid' for companies that would otherwise fail and disappear, taking with them precious jobs and export production capacity.

The workers proposed that they buy the factory using their redundancy settlements of approximately £1m, plus additional money from other, less clearly defined, sources. NVT agreed to allow the workers first refusal on the factory and equipment at Meriden, but reserved its right to reclaim the production tooling for the three-cylinder Trident. This was urgently needed to allow manufacture of the Trident to be completed entirely at the larger Small Heath factory. Previously Trident engine/gearbox units and other major components had been made at Small

Heath and shipped to Meriden for assembly in the Meriden-made frames. Unable to make the Trident frames without the drawings and tooling so securely locked inside Meriden, Trident production had stopped dead.

Desperate measures were called for and quickly applied. New drawings were made and the Small Heath factory re-tooled at a cost of £500,000. By April 1974, Small Heath was equipped for the manufacture of complete Tridents.

Around the world, motorcycle dealers were unable to get new Triumph machines or spare parts for their customers and many who dealt exclusively in Triumph faced bankruptcy.

By June 1974 the Triumph Trident was in production at Small Heath, where workers were sceptical about the confrontation at Meriden. Although Government ministers approved an outline proposal for a workers co-operative at Meriden producing an estimated 500 bikes per week, staff at Small Heath felt that the scheme would disproportionately benefit Meriden's 879 co-operative members at the expense of the rest of NVT employees. After thirteen months of negotiations and another general election on 10 October 1974 (the second that year) an initial agreement was reached and the stock of motorcycles began to move from Meriden into NVT's distribution network. T120 Bonnevilles released from Meriden between July and November of 1974 carry engine numbers in the series JJ 58080 to KJ 53067, and the liberated stocks of T140 versions run in the series KJ 59160 to NJ 60037.

In August the Lord Mayor of Coventry accompanied Tony Benn and his wife on a visit to Meriden. After touring the freshly-painted factory and speaking to the workers on the Government's industrial policy Benn departed to the strains of 'For he's a jolly fellow . . .'

The sit-in hit the shaky finances of NVT hard. No Government support could be secured for the company's two other factories at Small Heath and Wolverhampton where a total of 2,850 NVT staff continued to be employed in less confrontational circumstances. NVT consequently refused to sanction the Meriden Co-operative Agree-ment and formal redundancy notices were served on the staff barricaded in the factory. As a result the blockade was re-imposed on 24 November 1974.

NVT reconsidered the effects of the three-factory plan that was now in prospect. Management decided that to ensure the company reached profitability within five years an investment of £12m to £15m would be needed. Support of that order was seen as tantamount to the company being taken into public ownership. In exasperation, Dennis Poore stated the clear alternatives; a three-factory industry requiring Government finance to the tune of £15m or a two-factory industry without Meriden.

After a visit by Tony Benn to the Wolverhampton and Small Heath sites in November 1974, shop stewards were persuaded that the Government would offer support to NVT after the Meriden Co-operative had been set up.

When Trident production was shifted to Small Heath, management found that build quality dropped when non-craft tradespeople were used to assemble the bikes on a modernized, de-skilled, production line.

In this year Bert Hopwood retired and Sir Henry Ricardo, the inspired designer of the 1922 single-cylinder 500cc four-valve ohv Triumph Ricardo (the Riccy type IR fast roadster) died.

T140 Bonneville 1974

Production was stockpiled due to the factory blockade.

Commencing engine number GJ55101
Models: T120V Bonneville T120, T140V Bonneville T140, T140RV Bonneville T140

Engine
In spite of the shopfloor versus boardroom drama, the bike itself changed little. The flat rocker box inspection covers each gained two central set screw fixings and improved gaskets. The oil pressure release valve received gauze with a finer mesh and a new rubber-covered oil pressure sensor was fitted.

Home market 1974-version of the 74/75 US T140RV 750cc Bonneville. Finished in red with 'cold white' tank flashes the bike has chromed mudguards and is fitted with UK-type silencers instead of the stateside megaphone mufflers used for the US-export version.

UK and general export version of the 1974 T120V Bonneville 650cc five-speed. Purple slabsided tank with 'cold white' side flashes lined in gold, chromed mudguards and new, quieter, reverse cone silencers.

Transmission and Gearing

The gearbox sprocket outer face was chamfered to suit the new lockwasher and the 'O' ring oil seal that was now fitted to prevent oil seepage at the splines. A new plastic primary chaincase breather hose elbow replaced the previous metal fabrication.

Front Forks and Steering

The optional steering damper was no longer available.

Seat, Cycle Parts and Fittings

The colours purple and 'cold white' were available for the T120 and 'Cherokee red' and 'cold white' were used for the T140. Bonneville 650 and 750 side panel badges displayed standard gold lettering on black background.

US Specification Alternatives

For the US market, a 3.6 US gallon fuel tank was fitted.

1975 – THE STATE OF THE INDUSTRY

Model development of the Bonneville ceased during the troubled times of the Meriden blockade. Although assembly operations re-started during March 1975 using the stock of parts and the unfinished machines left over from the previous year, the models produced were identical to the 1974 Bonneville, with the only distinction being engine numbers. On 9 April the first bike to be wholly manufactured by the Workers Co-operative, a 1975 T140 with the engine number DK61000, was completed. Further 1974-specification machines were completed in 1975 and despatched between 10 March and early May. The T120s carried engine numbers up to NJ60070 and the T140s ran up to EK62239.

As the Meriden saga unfolded, stocks of fin-ished Nortons and Tridents were growing at the Wolverhampton and Small Heath factories. To export these bikes, NVT needed to be financially underwritten by the Government's Export Credit Guarantee Department. To provide NVT with guarantees beyond £4m, only slightly more than the value of the fast-growing stock already held, the ECGD would have to secure written approval from Mr Benn's Department of Indus-try, and to provide that, the Department of Industry would have to seek Parliamentary approval. The ultimate outcome of this was that, unless the rate of production was to be reduced, in a few short weeks NVT would have to tell its Small Heath factory to cease production if increased ECGD backing was not approved. The sting came when Tony Benn pointed out that if the Meriden proposals were agreed he would be

happy put a resolution to the House for the required additional export finance, enabling the Small Heath factory to continue in production beyond the £4m stock value level. Generously, he added that further Government investment in NVT might also be considered.

In this way the DTI was able to pressure NVT into making the Small Heath shop stewards an offer they could not refuse: drop your opposi-tion to the Meriden Co-operative or stop pro-duction at Small Heath. The Small Heath unions were left with no option but to lift their veto on the Meriden Co-operative, despite their firm belief that in so doing they were damaging the long-term interests of their members at Small Heath.

The Meriden Co-operative was officially rati-fied on 6 March 1975. Although the blockade formally ended on the same day, production had in fact been in progress since February in antici-pation of the final agreement now reached. Tony Benn greeted the news as a '. . . new chapter in the history of the motorcycle industry' Dennis Poore was less enthusiastic 'In the atmosphere of euphoria . . . I must strike a cautious note. This is, of course, an important milestone in the history of the industry and I would not like there to be any doubt about its significance. But I would be less than honest if I allowed it to be thought that we believe this outcome provides a sound, lasting and sensible solution to the industry's problems unless further substantial investment is provided.'

Factory equipment and tooling had been care-fully maintained pending this significant day and full-scale production was resumed smoothly. A Government loan of £4.8m further smoothed the way for the co-operative. Of this money, £3.9m was handed on to NVT. The Meriden Co-operative briefly became Synova Motors Limited before trading as the Meriden Motor Cycle Co-operative.

On the 25 June 1975 the last machine with the traditional right-side gear change was made ready for despatch. US standards dictated that gear change levers should be positioned on the left-hand side of the bike.

On 1 August 1975 the Government announced the withdrawal of the £4m Export Credit Guarantee Department Facility from NVT. This, plus the simultaneous cessation of any further financial support for NVT from the Government, finished NVT Engineering. Within a month the old Norton Villiers factory in Wolverhampton was placed in the hands of the liquidator and on 20 October a receiver was appointed for the NVT factory at Small Heath.

T140 Bonneville 1975

Price: unavailable
Commencing engine number DK61000
Model: T140 Bonneville 140

Specification
The specification of the bikes produced in 1975 was the same as for the 1974 model.

1976–77 – THE STATE OF THE INDUSTRY

After a 17-year production run, the 649cc Bonneville T120 was dropped from the 1976 Triumph range. Workers at the Meriden Co-op recognized that their dubious commercial prospects would be better served by the 744cc engine and its greater appeal in the US market. This single size of engine was to be produced at Meriden throughout the 1976 and 1977 seasons; the only variation on the 744cc T140 theme being the limited edition Jubilee model. The demands of the US market were the driving force behind the few modifications made during this period.

Despite its venerable engine design – perhaps even because of its venerable engine design – the Bonneville and its record of sporting achievement still held a strong attraction for American buyers. The hopes of all at the Meriden factory were dependant upon maintaining that attraction.

The Meriden Sales/Purchase Agreement made NVT the sole customer and distributor for all Meriden products until July 1977. During this period many key personnel were fired by Meriden Triumph. Top designers and some of the most experienced managers left the firm, taking essential experience with them. Inflationary prices increases were agreed between Meriden and NVT without conflict until the autumn of 1976, when NVT decided that any further price increases would be untenable. After seven months of intense negotiation the Government made a grant of £500,000 to enable the Co-op to buy the Triumph name from NVT along with the world-wide distribution and dealership rights. The severing of the contract, under which NVT bought 23,000 machines, came as a relief to both parties.

During the seven months of negotiations, production by the Meriden Co-operative had been progressing apace. During the early months of 1976 production reached 350 bikes per week.

Due to its insolvency resulting from the non-renewal of its ECGD funding, NVT was unable to collect, ship or distribute any of the machines produced at Meriden resulting in a backlog of over 3,000 machines held in stock at the factory. With a consequential cash-flow crisis imminent, the Co-op workers took the unprecedented step of laying themselves off work for five or six weeks whilst the problem was addressed. By 7 June 1976, NVT International was being wound up and Meriden was in urgent need of a large-scale customer.

A 'good fairy' in the unlikely shape of GEC stepped in to buy 2,000 motorcycles from Meriden and in doing so provided essential liquidity to the value of £1m. This enabled excess stock to be shifted and manufacturing to restart. Additionally, management advice on overseas and home marketing was made available to the Co-operative from Lord Stokes and Sir Arnold Weinstocks's GEC management team.

Dennis Poore indicated his intention to retreat from any further entanglement with Triumph.

The Isle of Man TT lost its World Championship race status.

T140 Bonneville 1976–77

Price: £874 (1976) and £1,012 (for T140V in 1977)
Commencing engine number HN62501 (1976); commencing engine number GP 75000 (1977)
Models: T140 Bonneville 140, T140 Bonneville 140 Jubilee

Engine

A new cylinder block was secured by UNF threaded studs and the washers previously fitted beneath the nuts at the cylinder base flange were deleted. The 8.6:1 compression ratio pistons could still be ordered but they were no longer fitted as standard specification; instead, 7.9:1 pistons became the norm. 'O' ring oil seals were introduced on the ignition timing plug in the primary chaincase and on the oil pressure release valve. The 30mm Concentric carburettors were now being produced at Amal's Spanish production facility, and extended float tickers and altered banjo union fibre washers were consequent detail changes. Induction noise was limited by new intake silencer tubes through each air filter element.

Transmission and Gearing

The most significant gearbox change was the move to left-foot gear selection. To enable the switch, new inner and outer gearbox covers with suitable joint washers were needed. The cross-over gear selector spindle had to include a crank to clear the clutch drum, but still of design necessity, the spindle emerged from the primary drive cover a little too far forward of the left footrest. A new spindle bush, revised gear change quadrant and a new kick-starter shaft were also required. To accommodate the re-positioned gear lever the primary-drive cover went without the alternator rotor inspection cover previously fitted; instead, a screwed-in inspection plug and fixed timing pointer were provided.

Frame and Rear Suspension

Provision of the new rear disc brake required a revised frame and swinging arm assembly. To allow for installation of the rear brake master cylinder and fluid reservoir under the seat, the ignition coil mounting platform and battery carrier were rearranged. The rider's footrests were produced in symmetrical form to allow the same component to serve on either side (previously individual left and right versions had been manufactured). The pillion footrests were made to fold at an upward angle of 45 degrees slanting rearwards, as required by US legislation.

Front Forks and Steering

There was no change to the forks but a knurled area, etched into the handlebars to provide additional grip for the front brake master cylinder clamp, entitled the bars to a new part number. The single rotor twistgrip resulted in the reintroduction of the in-line throttle cable splitter box.

Seat, Cycle Parts and Fittings

A new pressed steel seat pan was given more padding and covered in material with a finer grain effect. The seat hinges were rationalized to allow the same hinge component to be used for both the front and the rear seat fixing. The chromed front mudguards were not drilled to accept the front number plate mounting, as this was no longer a legal requirement in the UK. The twin front mudguard braces were deleted in favour of the earlier T150 Trident type bridge brace. The rear mudguard was slightly modified to clear the new rear disc brake. The plastic air filter covers bolted from the outside and the filter elements were pierced to fit on the new air intake tubes. New petrol taps were fitted showing on/off and reserve positions, as required by US legislation.

Electrics and Speedometer

The speedometer and tachometer received new faces without the NVT (Norton Villiers Triumph) logo.

The functions of the control console collar switches were now labelled; the left-side switch console function designations were cast into the switch body but the right-side switch had to make do with stick-on plastic labels. The ignition switch and headlamp-mounted warning lights carried similar stickers. New lenses for the indicators and the stop and tail lights were fitted, but remained interchangeable.

Wheels, Tyres and Brakes

To accommodate the new 10in diameter cast iron rear disc brake, a completely new rear hub was introduced and the brake pedal provided with a new pivot on the right-hand rear engine plate. The brake fluid reservoir was squeezed in under the seat by careful rearrangement of the electrical components. The front brake disc thickness was reduced to match the dimensions of the new rear disc.

1977 – THE STATE OF THE INDUSTRY

Thanks to the severing of the Meriden Sales/Purchase Agreement with NVT, Meriden was able to take-over the marketing of the Bonneville, Tiger 750 and Jubilee models from mid-season 1977 onwards.

After ECGD funds were denied and further Government funding withheld, NVT was left bankrupt and forced to stop production of the Triumph Trident at Small Heath.

Technically the 1977 Bonneville was unchanged from the previous year's model. For the first time a choice of colour schemes and detailed variations in finish were offered on the standard T140V. It could be ordered in either the new 'polychromatic blue' and white or the previous year's 'Cherokee red' and white,

At extra cost buyers could consider an alternative in the shape of the limited edition 'Silver Jubilee' Bonneville T140J, introduced to celebrate the 25th anniversary of Queen Elizabeth II's reign. Each model came with a certificate of authenticity and was finished in a suitably patriotic red, white and blue on a silver background. The original intention had been to limit production to a claimed 1,000; consequently each machine carries the proud boast of: 'One in a Thousand'.

However, when demand for the Silver Jubilee model persisted, a further 1,000 T140Js were run off. These were intended for transatlantic dealers and carried a less specific declaration of 'Limited Edition' on each flank. What might have been called 'fraud' had it been discovered in the auction houses of the art world was compounded when an additional batch of approximately 400 Jubilee Bonnevilles were produced for general export. The legend 'One in about Two and a Half Thousand' was not used; although it might have been more accurate, it did not have quite the same ring of authenticity.

T140J 'Silver Jubilee' Bonneville 1977

Price: £1,245

Engine

The Silver Jubilee Bonneville engine differed from the standard unit in appearance only. The aluminium alloy timing cover, gearbox outer cover and primary-drive chaincase were given a bright, chromium plate finish. Many Jubilee Bonnies were destined for an easy life as collectors' pieces, which was perhaps just as well because in anything less than ideal conditions the delicate finish applied to the engine covers could quickly deteriorate. Jubilee Bonneville engine numbers followed the same sequence as the standard T140V but included a 'J' suffix in place of the standard model's 'V'.

Transmission and Gearing

These were the same as for the standard T140V.

Frame and Rear Suspension

'Upside down', that is, fitted with the pre-load adjuster at the top, Girling gas-filled rear shock absorbers made their debut on the Jubilee Bonneville. Like the usual oil-filled units fitted to the standard T140V, the Jubilee's shockers had chromed springs.

Front Forks and Steering

Jubilee forks were distinguished by chromed top shrouds, which was the only variation from the standard 1976 version of the forks.

The 1977 T140J Silver Jubilee Bonneville engine differed from the standard unit in appearance only. The aluminium alloy timing cover, gearbox outer cover and primary-drive chaincase were given a bright, chromium plate finish. However, in anything less than ideal conditions, the delicate finish on the engine covers could quickly deteriorate.

Seat, Cycle Parts and Fittings

The cycle parts for the Jubilee only differed from standard in terms of colour and finish. Instead of being chromed the mudguards were painted in the Silver Jubilee theme colours, a blue centre stripe enclosed by white and red lining on a silver background. The UK Jubilee 'breadbin' tank carried a blue styling panel surrounded by red and white lining on the silver background. In the US, the limited edition Jubilee was fitted with the 3.6 US gallon round tank finished in the same colours. On the Jubilee's dualseat the red, blue and silver theme continued. The blue seat cover was set off by red piping following a revised pattern around the seat top and a chromed rim trim finished off the lower edge. This same seat would later be manufactured in more restrained colours and become a standard fitment on all Bonnevilles.

Beneath the seat new silver side panels carried screw-fixed 'Bonneville 750' badges accompanied by a stick-on plastic label in red, white and blue. The label showed a Union Jack flanked by the 'Silver Jubilee' title and either the initial claim of 'One in a Thousand' or the later, less specific, declaration of 'Limited Edition'. Like the seat, the Jubilee's updated side panels would later be produced in more workaday colours and become a feature of the standard Bonnie.

Wheels, Tyres and Brakes

Each chrome wheelrim was painted with a blue central band lined in red and white. The Jubilee's tyres were Dunlop K91 4.10 × 19in at the front and Red Arrow 4.10 × 18in at the rear.

Perhaps the 1977 T140V was never intended as a 'ride to work' machine. In everyday use the delicate bright work faded and the paint rapidly lost its lustre.

1977 750cc T140V Bonneville 140 Jubilee limited edition celebrating the 25th Jubilee year of Queen Elizabeth II.

1978 – THE STATE OF THE INDUSTRY

Scott Motorcycles ceased production.

Stocks of Triumph machines piled up due to price increases resulting from the strength of sterling against the US dollar. In response, staffing levels at Meriden were cut by 150 to 600, a three-day working week was invoked and production reduced to 200 machines per week.

Incredibly, the successful but modest Rickman concern, specialists in race preparation and after-market motorcycle accessory manufacture, now became the UK's second largest motorcycle manufacturer.

The Triumph's US catalogue defiantly declared 'The Legend Lives on'.

T140 Bonneville 1978

Price: £1,284
Commencing engine number HX 00100
Models: T140V Bonneville 140, T140E Bonneville 140

Engine

The reduced 7.9:1 compression ratio was made standard for all export markets. The halcyon days of the Bonneville's 'fastest bike in town' image were long gone and the factory turned vice into virtue by emphasizing the improved reliability derived from a lower state of tune. More mature considerations now took on an increased priority. Other changes during this final year for Meriden's T140V included a new composite head gasket to replace the original solid copper version and, from engine number 02690, rocker arms and adjusters with UNF threads. A serrated lockwasher was also introduced beneath the crankshaft rotor nut, and the thrust washer behind the tacho drive gear was modified to prevent possible breakage.

By January 1978 the focus of the export-driven production schedule had shifted away from the T140V to the T140E, a machine with reduced toxic emissions destined for the environmentally regulated US market. The E in the T140E stood for Emissions Compliance, as regulated by the US Environmental Protection Agency (EPA). The transition marked the end of a cherished Bonneville icon, the splayed port cylinder head. On the T140E's new head casting parallel inlet tracts with stub mounts supported new Amal 'Mark 2' Concentric carburettors. Iron valve guides secured in position by circlips and revised valve spring bottom cups were also featured as part of the new cylinder head specification. The 'Mark 2' Concentric carburettors featured a cleaner running integral cold-start mechanism with a control lever assembly on the left-hand carb body. This allowed the previous model's twin control cables and handlebar-mounted choke lever to be dispensed with.

EPA directives specified a closed circuit engine breather system, that is, the engine vented crankcase gas through the primary-drive chaincase into the induction airbox, not to atmosphere as before. In the same way, the oil tank breather was redirected to the exhaust rockerbox.

Transmission and Gearing

A gasket was introduced between the inner and outer covers of the gearbox.

Frame and Rear Suspension

The frame was unchanged but safety-related revisions were made to the mounting bolt arrangement of the pillion footrests. As a result, specific left and right side footpegs again had to be manufactured. A midseason upgrade saw the Bonneville's hydraulic rear suspension units replaced with the gas-filled units first seen on the previous year's Jubilee Bonneville.

Front Forks and Steering

A self-aligning fork oil seal and retainer were introduced and made available for retro fitting to earlier (post-1970) forks. UK and general export models were treated to the chrome upper fork shrouds previously reserved for US exports.

Seat, Cycle Parts and Fittings

Less colourful, toned down, versions of the Silver Jubilee seat were fitted to all Bonnevilles. To suit

1978 T140V Bonneville, with high-rise handlebars and plenty of chrome. This machine has been completed to the US specification but was intended for use in the UK. US-export models went without the rubber gaiters on the front fork.

1978 T140V Bonneville, assembled to the UK specification. Any version could be supplied to customers regardless of their location.

Engine detail of 1978 Bonneville fitted with the Mark 2 Amal Concentric carburettors, easily distinguished by their 'squarer' appearance.

the alternative US and UK fuel tank styles, two versions of the seat were made available: narrow nose to suit the US 'round' tank, or broad nose for the wider UK 'breadbin'. Seat covers were black or brown, dependent on the bike's chosen colour scheme, and both sported the Triumph logo on the rear panel. Jubilee-type side panels were introduced on all Bonnevilles, this time with additional support provided by a concealed fixing spring located on the back of each panel.

Electrics and Instruments
Lighting was improved by the provision of a Lucas 45/40W headlamp powered by a cheaper Yuasa 12N9 4B1 battery. The stop and tail lamp unit was polished and protected with a clear lacquer finish. In the main, Smith's instruments continued to be fitted but French-made Veglia speedometers and tachometers were used to

overcome occasional but increasingly frequent supply difficulties.

Wheels, Tyres and Brakes
The front wheel gained sealed bearings and the rear received a new rim to suit the tougher 9-gauge spokes and nipples that were also fitted. This strengthened wheel was better able to cope with the increased stresses imposed by the disc brake introduced on the 1976 model.

1979 – THE STATE OF THE INDUSTRY

The Bonneville won the *Motor Cycle News* 'Machine of The Year' award, possibly presented as a late recognition of the bike's earlier achievements rather than its current market position.

Geoffrey Robinson, Labour MP for Coventry North West and former chief Executive of Jaguar

Cars, took the unpaid role of chief executive at Triumph. His prime concern was finding a well-heeled partner for the company but, sadly, he was unsuccessful.

Japanese competition was fierce.

T140 Bonneville 1979

Price: £1,577
Commencing engine number HA11001
Models: T140E Bonneville, T140D Bonneville 'Special'

Engine

The Phillips-head screws securing engine outer covers were replaced by Allen-type bolts; a move much anticipated by true enthusiasts over the previous twenty years. Apart from the fitting of a timing cover gasket, the T140E (for Emissions) engine continued for the most part unchanged into 1979. The black-painted engine of the newly introduced T140D Special shared the T140E cylinder head and in addition featured a siamesed, two-into-one exhaust system. This discharged through a unique tapered silencer mounted on the right-hand side of the bike. Horizontal finning on the timing plate cover indicated the installation of Lucas electronic ignition.

Transmission and Gearing

Both the T140E and T140D had a raised button on the gear selector camplate to operate a green 'neutral selected' warning lamp. In addition, the depth of the neutral notch in the camplate was increased to provide a more positive location.

Frame and Rear Suspension

Girling gas shock absorbers remained standard fitments for all models. The rubber-mounted

A US-specification Bonneville nears the end of the production line.

That most essential item of the assembly line equipment, the tea mug stands ready for action on the workbench as another machine is prepared for US export.

A steady hand and a cool eye were pre-requisites for tank lining at Meriden. The tank flash being lined is the 'swept wing' pattern used in the 1979–80 season.

Crankshafts ready for engine assembly on the Bonneville production line.

The 1979 Bonneville T140D with high-rise handlebars, light alloy wheels and, unique in the Triumph range, a Siamesed, two-into-one, exhaust system.

The 1979 T140D 'Special', finished in black with gold striping. The T140D featured a unique two-into-one exhaust system. The model represented a significant departure from traditional Triumph styling without the need for costly design revisions. Both US and UK versions were fitted with chrome-plated mudguards front and rear.

footrest rubbers were re-profiled with a flat-topped tread area, a squarer section and chamfered outer ends. As a result of the more complex profile, the new rubbers had to be produced in left and right-handed versions. The hinged seat was fitted with a security lock and, on T140Vs, a small chromed luggage rack was incorporated as part of the rear mudguard stay. On the T140D Special the tiny but decorative parcel rack was replaced by a grab rail and the swing arm modified to allow the fitting of a Dunlop TT100 4.25 × 18in rear tyre. The footrests were lifted by two inches and the centre stand modified to provide maximum ground clearance for the D Special's single silencer. In spite of this, the T140D's cornering ability continued to be limited by the exhaust when taking right handers.

Front Forks and Steering

Slight modifications were made to accommodate the repositioned steering lock, now located on the bottom yoke to allow for the fitting of a warning lamp panel and ignition switch at the top of the forks. On the D Special the lower brace of the front mudguard was deleted and the fork adapted to accept the Lester cast alloy wheel.

New handlebars and offset fulcrum 'dog leg' control levers were introduced to match the handlebar-mounted switch consoles. For UK models a right-hand rear view mirror was made standard equipment.

Detailed engine shot of a T140D 'Special' showing the Siamesed pipes, Mark 2 Amal Concentric carbs and the electric starter motor.

Cycle Parts, Seat and Fittings

On UK and general export fuel tanks the rubber knee grips were dropped. The T140D Special was fitted with a new seat featuring a higher pillion riding position but still constructed on the old seat pan. UK and US T140Es were fitted with the same chrome-plated mudguards as the previous year, but the T140D Special sported shorter mudguard blades, still chrome plated but less efficient than the full-size T140E mudguard. US specification models could now be ordered for use on UK roads, and by the same token many specially ordered UK-spec machines were to be seen on American highways.

Electrics and Instruments

From the start of 1979, Lucas Rita electronic ignition became standard equipment for the Bonneville. Further electrical upgrades were the installation of a 10.5A RM24 three-phase alternator with 3DS rectifier, a change to negative earth electrics and a new ZD715 Zener diode mounted on the aluminium induction filter. The sender unit for the new ignition system was mounted in the points compartment in the timing chest and protected by a finned alloy cover, black on the T140D and polished alloy on the T140E. Timing was adjusted by shifting the back plate after loosening the two clamping screws. The sender unit controlled an AB11 amplifier unit located under the seat behind the right-hand side panel. The ignition switch and four warning lights, one each for indicators, neutral selected, high beam and oil pressure, shared a central panel mounted between the French-made Veglia speedo and tachometer.

Wheels, Tyres and Brakes

10in diameter discs controlled by Lockheed calipers were fitted front and rear. The front brake was given a handlebar-mounted master cylinder to blend with the updated switch consoles. On the T140E the wheel hubs were polished and finished with clear lacquer. Rear tyre size was increased briefly to 4.25 × 18in but restored to the earlier 4.10 × 18in after clearance problems were experienced when carrying pillion passengers. The T140D rear brake caliper was mounted on a plate above the swing arm fork. The T140D Special ran on its show stopping seven-spoke cast alloy wheels, finished in black with polished alloy edges on rim and spokes. These US-made Lester wheels oozed with hi-tech state of the art perfection and to prove it, each wheel came with a certified X-ray examination certificate that placed the component's structural integrity beyond doubt.

US Specifications/Options/Alternatives

Customer preference increasingly dictated specification. The only constraint became suitability for use; apart from that, what the customer wanted, the customer got.

9 The Decline

1980 – THE STATE OF THE INDUSTRY

Triumph's US success story finally went 'pear shaped'. With 1979 Bonnies lying unsold in American showrooms and warehouses, the home market at last assumed a greater significance to the factory.

The engineering design efforts of Brian Jones came to fruition when the T140 ES Electric Start version of the Bonneville was introduced on 2 April 1980.

In August 1980 the Bonneville T140ES, Tiger 750 and a 'Low Rider' Bonneville, a design concept model for the US market, featured on Triumph's stand at the Earl's Court show. Market intelligence gathered at the show was promising but, sadly, at the factory a different situation existed. A 'mass' meeting of the remaining 450 staff was told the current output of 45 to 50 machines per week could be produced by 150 workers if full-time working were resumed. It

On 9 August 1980 popular support for Triumph is demonstrated by members of the Triumph Owners Club in Whitehall as they head for Downing Street with a petition against the closure of Meriden.

A prototype 'Low Rider' Bonneville, a design concept model for the US market, featured on Triumph's stand at the 1980 Earl's Court show. The reception at the show was promising but, sadly, at the factory a different situation existed.

was proposed that the surplus 300 staff members take voluntary redundancy and put an end to the inefficient short working week.

Total Meriden debt reached over £6m as a further £2m was added to the original £4.2m loan extended in 1975. Eventually the total debt grew to £7m before being written off by the Government in late September 1980. As a further gesture of good faith, a remaining £4m still owed to the Export Credit Guarantee Department would be considered liquidated if Triumph were able to raise £2m towards the outstanding amount by selling machines stockpiled in the US. Without question, Triumph raised the required £2m and settled the debt.

Both Government and the company recognized that without the write-offs Meriden would not have been able to repay the sums outstanding. Geoffrey Robinson observed that 'We now have a clean slate and the most secure financial position for five years' and promptly stood down as chief executive.

Triumph continued with experimental designs, but none could offer a solution to the company's terminal state.

T140 Bonneville 1980

Price: £1,797 (T140ES Bonneville Electro) and £1,897 (T140E Bonneville Executive)
Commencing engine number PB25001 and T140ES (electric start) CB29901
Models: T140E Bonneville, T140ES Bonneville (Electric Start), T140D Bonneville 'Special'

Engine
1980 was a year of significant change, but the valve guides, carburettor mounts, engine breather system and cylinder head configuration continued as in the previous year. The oil pump was equipped with secondary check ball valves in both the feed and scavenge circuits, an improvement that required a larger oil pump body with additional chambers. Consequently a larger timing-cover casting was introduced to provide the necessary increased accommodation. A front pipe mounting modification gave the silencers a slightly upswept style.

From April 1980, an electric start Bonneville became available. The T140ES offered a 12V Lucas M3 starter motor as a belated response to what had become a standard feature of many Japanese models. The Lucas starter motor was positioned beneath the Amal Mark II Concentric carburettors, where the pre-unit Triumph twin engine had carried the magneto. It drove through a 20:1 reduction ratio. The starter nose projected into the timing chest to mate with the inlet gear train via a pinion equipped with a Borg-Warner sprag clutch. This pinion ran on bushes fitted into new crankcase and timing cover castings and a removable section of the outer timing cover allowed maintenance access.

Although the starter motor position meant that Top Dead Centre (TCC) location arrangement could not be used, and a series of modifications would be required before the various in-service snags were finally overcome, the Bonneville was at last able to match the competition with an electric starter.

Transmission and Gearing
A revised primary-drive chain tensioner enabled the chain to be tensioned without draining the transmission lubricant.

Frame and Rear Suspension
From late 1979 additional brackets had been fitted to the frame in anticipation of the installation of solenoid equipment for the new electric starter.

The 1980 T140E Bonneville for the US market. The 'Olympic flame' fuel tank had black side flashes lined with gold above and below the tank badges. The transparent brake fluid reservoir demanded by US safety legislation allowed the fluid level to be easily monitored.

The rear swinging arm fork was rationalized to allow it to be manufactured using a common symmetrical component to form both left and right-hand fork legs. The outside tube diameter was increased from 32mm to 38mm. A heavier chain tensioner and improved brake caliper torque stay were also incorporated into the new swinging arm. Pillion footrests were lifted to provide clearance for the higher exhaust system after a front pipe alteration gave the silencers a more upswept style. The battery box was enlarged to accommodate the bigger battery that would be needed later in the production year when the T140ES Electric Start models appeared.

The UK version of the T140D Special was fitted with the same exhaust set up as the T140E twin. Only in the US did the D Special two-into-one Siamese system survive.

Front Forks and Steering

The fork slider middle lug and the fork stem were modified to accommodate the updated Neiman anti-theft steering lock. Other components remained interchangeable.

Seat, Cycle Parts and Fittings

The seat pan pressing was modified to provide additional space for the larger YB14L battery. Positive stops incorporated in the twinseat hinges rendered the seat check strap redundant. New side panels covered the air filter box and housed the electronic ignition; on the right-hand panel a small window enabled visual inspection of fluid level in the re-sited rear brake reservoir.

Electrics and Instruments

To counter vibration damage the indicators were protected by rubber mounts. The trigger coils and AB11 ignition amplifier were re-configured to produce a more intense spark at lower revs to improve initial firing, an early problem on ES and D electric start models. The green starter button was mounted on the right handlebar beneath the engine kill switch. A 14A Lucas RM24 three-phase alternator was specified and a larger capac-ity Yuasa YB14L battery introduced. The ZD715 Zener diode was deleted in favour of a three-pack Zener diode array wired to, and directly controlling, each of the three phases of alternator output. Kick-started versions of the Bonneville soldiered on with the 12N9-4B1 battery and the old 10.5A stator assembly.

By 1980 Smith's instruments were no longer in production. Provision was consequently dis-continued and Veglia speedometers and tachometers became the standard fitments for the Bonneville; another Britbike icon lost.

Wheels, Tyres and Brakes

The rear brake caliper for all models was shifted to the top-mounted position previously used on the T140D Special. As a result the torque stay was revised and the brake fluid reservoir re-sited behind the right-hand side panel. A stronger brake pedal was also fitted. The front brake fluid reservoir was manufactured in opaque plastic to enable the fluid level to be checked without removing the cap. The Veglia speedometer drive gearbox was moved from the left to the right-hand side of the rear wheel. A new rear hub was provided to accommodate the change along with a thinner disc brake rotor and shorter disc bolts.

The previous 4.10 × 19in front and 4.10 × 18in rear wheels and tyres continued. The D Special rode on into 1980 with its 4.10 × 19in front and 4.25 × 18in rear Lester cast alloy wheels. Dunlop gave way to Avon Roadrunner tyres as original equipment.

Fuel Supply

New fuel taps were fitted to reduce potential leaks.

US Specifications/Options/Alternatives

US specification and UK and general (now known as ROW, rest of the world) export models were made available to customers regardless of their intended market or country of destination.

1981 – THE STATE OF THE INDUSTRY

The UK industry contracted still further, with motorcycle news becoming ever more sparse.

Hesketh motorcycles launched their new V-twin, but the under-funded company failed soon after. Triumph re-introduced the Thunderbird, a name not seen since 1966. Designated the TR65, the Thunderbird was the only 650cc bike in the Triumph range.

Well founded rumours of an eight-valve Bonneville started to circulate. In fact the bike, the TSS, was being planned but did not appear until 1982, too late to avert Triumph's inevitable demise.

T140 Bonneville 1981

Price: £1,965.52 (750cc kick-start), £2,035.53 (Electro), and £2,422.18 (Executive Electro)
Commencing engine number KDA28001
Models: T140E Bonneville, T140ES Bonneville (Electric Start), T140E Bonneville Executive, T140ES Executive (Electric Start), T140AV Bonneville (Anti-Vibration Police Version)

Engine

To improve access during servicing the Top Dead Centre (TDC) location sleeve was, as in 1968, again moved to the front of the right-hand timing side crankcase. Although inconvenient this position avoided the obstruction presented by the starter motor on T140ES models. The corresponding crankshaft TDC and 38 degrees before Top Dead Centre notches were re-sited to accordingly.

Another theme from previous years reintroduced for 1981 was the push-over exhaust front pipe. For the new season these were again secured to the screwed-in exhaust stubs by finned ring clamps.

The drive-side main bearing remained unaltered but on the timing side the bearing was upgraded to a four-lipped heavy-duty roller. At the top end, new valve guides allowed the fitting of inlet valve stem oil seals. The inlet and exhaust cam followers and guide blocks were made a common component and at the same time the exhaust tappet cam follower oil pressure feed was deleted.

On the police specification anti-vibration model the crankcases were modified to suit

The 1981 T140ES 750cc Bonneville European with optional electric start. On this bike the 4 gallon (Imperial) 'breadbin' tank is finished in 'smokey flame' with gold lining. The mudguards are stainless steel.

revised rubber-insulated engine mounts and the crankshaft was re-engineered to the 55 per cent balance factor.

Although early 1981 E and ES models destined for America were despatched with Amal Mark II Concentric carburettors, later in the year these were replaced by German Bing 32mm Type 94 constant vacuum carburettors. To protect the vulnerable exposed linkages on the Bing carburettors the outer side panels were extended forwards. The early Amal Mark II Concentrics fitted to US exports had larger needle jets and were equipped with cable-operated chokes controlled from the right handlebar In the less stringently controlled UK, the Amal Mark II Concentrics remained as standard equipment on all but the Executive models.

Transmission and Gearing

The clutch plates were reduced in thickness by one gauge to allow the fitting of a cork insert at the back of the clutch drum and the inclusion of seven plain plates and six driven plates. The changes allowed the use of lighter T120 clutch springs without any loss of efficiency.

Frame and Rear Suspension

The modified frame introduced the previous year continued unchanged and now formed the basis for both the electric and kick-started versions of the Bonneville. The Police Service T140AV featured a frame equipped with rubber-bushed anti-vibration engine mounts. Manufacture of gas suspension units was now under threat as Girling reviewed the economics of low volume production. A search was begun for a suitable replacement as supplies would run out before the end of the 1981 season.

Front Forks and Steering

Grooves were cut into the outer members to provide more positive circlip location of the fork seals.

Cycle Parts and Fittings

The UK 4 gallon tank and 3.6 US gallon tank continued with a wider choice of colours. The US models were fitted with locking fuel tank filler caps. Stainless steel front and rear mudguards were introduced for 1981. However, on the Executive package painted mudguards were retained to complement the smoke-effect tank finish. Side panels for all colour schemes apart from the Executive were black with chrome on black badging.

As the 1981 season progressed the supply of traditional British-made tanks tapered off, and so alternatives were sourced from Italy and fitted to the Executive. The $4\frac{1}{2}$ gallon Italian tanks featured the old central mounting, a new flip-up filler cap and a plain Triumph name badge as used on UK and 'Rest of the World' machines. US tanks wore the eyebrow-style tank badge.

The T140E and ES versions could be ordered with an Executive package that brought a fork-mounted cockpit fairing and a colour co-ordinated set of quickly detachable panniers and top box. The luggage, fairing and side panels were supplied in matching shades of 'smokey red' or 'smokey blue'. The interior of the fairing was finished in a leather-grain effect reproduced in plastic, and round driving mirrors were attached on each side.

Seat

One of five versions of the seat were provided. The type of seat fitted depended upon the model's US or UK specification, which fuel tank was fitted and whether the bike was an electric or kick-start version. Most E and ES versions were equipped with the stepped-type seat introduced on the T140D Special. The US-specification 'Executive' featured the fifth variation; a stepped 'King and Queen' twinseat featuring a defining ridge at the rear of the rider's section and a raised pillion section.

Wheels, Tyres and Brakes

The Lester cast alloy wheels unique to the T140D Special were replaced by Morris wheels and from 1981 could be specified for any Bonneville. Like the Lester items, Morris alloy wheels were finished in black with a polished finish highlighting spoke details and rim edges. Late in the season, twin-disc front brakes were made available; first on the Executive, then throughout the range.

1982 – THE STATE OF THE INDUSTRY

An eight-valve modification for the TSS cylinder head was negotiated with Weslake, the respected engine specialists.

Triumph had first produced a four valve per cylinder engine in 1924 for the 500cc Type IR Ricardo Roadster. Cylinder head design and development for the record-breaking 500cc 'Riccy' had been undertaken by combustion chamber specialists Ricardo and Company Ltd under the personal supervision of Henry Ricardo, later to become Sir Henry in recognition for his services to the motor industry. Nearly sixty years on, Meriden turned to the engine tuners Weslake for another four valve per cylinder, off the shelf performance package; this time for the Bonneville.

For nearly fifteen years Weslake had been offering a four valve per cylinder high performance conversion for the 650cc and 750cc Triumph twins. Meriden, by now desperate to squeeze extra power from the ageing Bonneville motor but without the cash needed to fund development, sought technical advice from Weslake. They proposed a factory-produced version of Weslake's already proven multi-valve engine. The resulting T140W TSS featured the eight-valve head combined with a radically redesigned crankshaft and flywheel forging that was capable of running at 10,000rpm.

The Meriden operation was now a pale shadow of its former self. The small remaining workforce produced the company's limited output from a building at the rear of the Meriden works. Plans to sell the 22 acre factory site for residential development were afoot and a move to Coventry, the location of Triumph's earliest

motorcycle factory, was considered. Coincidentally, the relocation plan, initiated for reasons of economy, would take Triumph Motorcycles to Cash's Lane, Foleshill Road; the same location used by Triumph cars after the 1936 company split.

In the autumn of 1982 more rumours did the rounds, this time of the possible development of an all-new water-cooled, four valve per cylinder twin-cylinder engine with double overhead camshafts.

T140 Bonneville 1982

Price: £2,025 (T140E), £2,075 (T140E Electro)
Commencing engine number HDA30651 (8 July 1981)
Models: T140E Bonneville, T140ES Bonneville Electric Start, T140E and ES Executive, T140LE Bonneville Royal (Limited Edition)

Engine
Electric start modifications were consolidated and the 1981 engine continued unchanged into 1982.

Transmission and Gearing
Primary drive changes made in the previous year continued unaltered. There were no changes to the gearbox. The rear wheel sprocket was reduced in size from 47 to 45 teeth.

Frame and Rear Suspension
As the last stocks of Girling shock absorbers dwindled away, the Marzocchi suspension units first made available exclusively for the US market was made a standard fitting for all Bonnevilles. The Limited Edition Royal Wedding version was produced in two distinct versions, UK and US. The UK models had a silver frame.

Front Forks and Steering
Black fork sliders were fitted on all UK Bonnies, even the Limited Edition Royal; the single exception was the top of the range Royal deluxe which had polished fork legs. All forks were equipped to accommodate the twin disc brake,

The 1982 limited edition T140LE Bonneville Royal. The UK model shown here had an all-black engine and a grey painted frame; the US-export version stayed with a more conventional polished engine in a black painted frame.

whether fitted or not. Headlamp brackets were rubber mounted and US models were fitted with 6½in rise bars, the same as UK machines. Ironically only the UK market 'Electro USA' variant now had the 8½in high-rise US-style handlebars.

Cycle Parts and Fittings
The 4 gallon fuel tank initially introduced on the 1981 Bonneville Executive was adopted across the range. The optional 3.6 US gallon tank remained available and shared the 'flip-up' filler cap. The executive came with small or large fairing, painted guards, panniers and top box in red or black with colour-matched styling panels.

Electrics and Speedometer
A more powerful 60/45W sealed-beam head-lamp unit was fitted. Durable ULO direction indicators were fitted at front and rear. The Veglia speedometer and rev counter continued.

Wheels, Tyres and Brakes
The optional Morris cast alloy wheels became standard fitment on the T140ES model; from this time on the ES would be known as the Electro. Sintered 'all-weather' Dunlop brake pads, Lock-heed alloy brake calipers and smaller 9.8in discs were all made standard equipment across the Bonneville range. Twin front discs, a standard feature on the Bonneville Executive, were made

available as an option on all models. Buyers of the T140LE deluxe who opted for spoked wheels were obliged to accept a single-disc brake set-up.

US Specifications/Options/Alternatives

Traditional spoked wheels with chrome rims were offered as an option to US buyers.

1983 – THE STATE OF THE INDUSTRY

The 60bhp TSS, with its eight-valve engine and new crankshaft, proved to be a flyer. Capable of 130mph but compromised by the poor quality of the bought-in engine block and cylinder head castings, the bike came too late to change the factory's dire financial situation.

The rumoured 'Phoenix' model failed to appear. First heard of in the late autumn of the previous year, this proposed new engine was described as a water-cooled DOHC twin-cylinder engine with four valve per cylinder combustion chambers. The new motor, the first all-new engine since the Speed Twin of 1937, was even featured at the Birmingham Show in March

Some things never go out of fashion and the Triumph Bonneville is one of them. The Bonneville featured here is the production version of the 'Low Rider' concept bike shown at the 1980 show: the 1983 TSX. Mechanically it was identical to the T140ES, but benefited from the large-bore exhaust system and the 16in rear wheel with its fat section Avon Roadrunner tyre.

A rare shot of the elusive Phoenix, shows a mock up of the completed bike placed in an inaccessible part of Triumph's stand at the 1983 Birmingham Motorcycle Show. The remote location of the bike may have been intended to discourage closer inspection.

1983. Sadly, the show engine and a mocked-up exhibit of a complete bike were to be the only tantalizing glimpses of the phantom machine.

The last Meriden Bonnie was built on 7 January 1983, engine number AEA34389.

Triumph Motorcycles (Meriden) Ltd went into voluntary liquidation on 26 August 1983.

The Bonneville was offered the chance of an after life thanks to property developer John Bloor. Initially only interested in the redevelopment potential of the Meriden factory site, Bloor subsequently took an interest in the Triumph name, backed that interest with cash and outbid established motorcycle industry contenders to secure the manufacturing rights.

Hesketh Motorcycles was re-financed, but again failed after producing forty 'Vampire' machines.

The 'Phoenix' motor. First heard of in the late autumn of 1982, this engine was described as a water-cooled DOHC twin with four valves per cylinder. The new motor, the first all-new engine since the Speed Twin of 1937, was featured at the Birmingham Show in March 1983. Sadly, the show engine and the mocked-up exhibit of a complete bike were to be the only tantalizing glimpses of the proposed machine.

Ultimately, the battle was lost and in 1984 Triumph's Meriden factory was demolished to make way for new residential property. Bonneville Close and Daytona Drive are among the addresses which now occupy the site.

T140E Bonneville 1983

Engine

In the face of overwhelming financial difficulties the T140E and the ES boldly continued in production. Minor changes were made to the starter motor drive pinion. The newly introduced TSX had the T140ES engine with black rocker boxes and cylinder head; cooling fin edges were polished to emphasize the high-tech image and a $1\frac{3}{4}$in large bore exhaust system was produced exclusively for the model. After engine number GEA33965 the TSX was equipped with pistons giving a 7.4 to 1 compression ratio instead of the 7.9 to 1 pistons fitted to the two valve per cylinder range.

The TSS's one-piece forged crankshaft featured 1.875in diameter big end journals, thicker flywheel webs and high specification roller main bearings. Bores of the new engine were spaced $\frac{1}{2}$ in further apart than standard and required the connecting rods to run slightly off centre on the small end gudgeon pins. Flat-topped 9.5 to 1 pistons had four valve clearance pockets machined in the crowns and ran in steel liners. The traditional head gasket was replaced by two

separate cross-ring seals located in the mating face of the cylinder head. A total of ten bolts secured the head with the four outer bolts running straight through the cylinder block casting to thread into the crankcase.

Camshaft timing was tweaked to take full advantage of the improved breathing available through the eight valves. In the UK the engine was fitted with 34mm Bing carburettors but local emissions legislation limited the US version to 32mm carburettors.

The new eight-valve head and cylinder castings featured integral rocker boxes and bolt-up exhaust pipe flanges sealed by gas-tight rings. Two full-width rocker box covers were secured by Allen bolts and housed forked rocker arms, each operating its own pair of valves. These were grouped around a central 10mm spark plug and inclined at 30 degrees. The same combination of camshafts specified for the TSS, mild inlet and fierce exhaust, operated each pair of valves through modified T140 push rods.

The TSS offered a top speed of 125mph and, with its new black finish crankcases, cylinder head and barrel contrasting with the polished outer covers and cooling fin edges, it looked

The 1983 Triumph T140W TSS eight valve, easily recognised by the radical multi-valve cylinder head. The poor quality of the bought-in head casting was a cause for concern.

The 1983 TSX. High bars and the 16in rear wheel with its fat tyre gave the model 'custom' styling. The T140ES engine with matt black rocker boxes and cylinder head had polished fin edges to emphasize the high-tech image.

1983 T140 TSX. Laid back 'Easy Rider' appeal for US taste at home or abroad.

T140E 740cc Bonneville 1983

Price: £2,204

Commencing engine number BEA 33001 (February 1982)

Models: T140E Bonneville, T140ES Bonneville (Electric Start), T140TSX £2,359 (GEA 33528 June 1982), T140 TSS £2,499 (CEA 33027 March 1982), T140 AV Executive £2,549 (GEA 33526 June 1982)

Engine

Cylinder bore	76mm
Stroke	82mm
Cylinder capacity	747cc
Compression ratio	7.9:1
Output	not declared

Carburettors

Type	Amal Concentric Mk2
Choke size	30mm
Main jet	200
Pilot jet	20
Needle	Type '2C3' (second position)
Needle jet	0.106

Fuel tank

Capacity	4 gallons (Imperial)

Gearbox (five speed)

Top	4.5:1
4th	5.36
3rd	6.3
2nd	8.27
1st	11.63

Electrics

Ignition	Lucas AB11 Electronic
Charging circuit	Lucas RM24 three-phase alternator charging through a 3DS rectifier and ZD 715 Zener Diode
Battery	YB14L
Spark plugs	N5 gapped at 0.25

Tyres

Front	4.10 × 19in
Rear	4.10 × 18in

Brakes

Front	9.8in single disc (twin disc optional)
Rear	9.8in single disc

Pre-assembly inspection of the eight-valve T140W TSS cylinder head in the early months of 1983. The TSS offered a top speed of 125mph (201km/h) and, with its new black finish cylinder head and barrel contrasting with the polished outer covers and cooling fin edges it looked good. The downside was poor build quality and low reliability resulting from porous cylinder head castings.

Close up of the TSS eight-valve engine. The unit was built around T140ES crankcase casting but the block and cylinder head were easily distinguished from the four-valve Bonnie. The side panels were finished in contrasting half matt, half gloss, black.

good. The downside was poor build quality and low reliability resulting from porous cylinder head castings.

Transmission and Gearing

On the TSS, the footrests were moved rearwards to provide a better high-speed riding position and this resulted in the provision of a remote gearchange linkage. From engine number DEA 33133 the gearbox mainshaft thread was revised from $\frac{5}{8}$ to $\frac{9}{16}$ and a new locking washer and self-locking nut specified. On the TSS, gear ratios were raised to take advantage of the extra power available from the eight-valve head. On the TSX, a 47-tooth rear sprocket allowed lower gearing to produce snappier acceleration.

Frame and Rear Suspension

The footrests were resited towards the rear on the TSS. The only other change came on the 'low rider' style TSX frame with a revised swinging arm to allow for the fitting of the Brembo rear brake cylinder bracket and wider section rear tyre. The TSX and T140E were fitted with Paioli rear suspension units and the TSS had Marzocchi 'Strada' units.

Front Forks and Steering

The front forks were the same as before but now fitted with black rubber gaiters. The TSX had a polished top yoke and sliders.

Cycle Parts and Fittings

Self-adhesive decorative decals were applied to the painted fuel tanks and the TSX benefited from a completely new fuel tank with centrally mounted filler cap, single fuel tap and balance pipe. Locking fuel caps were a standard fitment for the US and available at extra cost on UK models. Polished stainless steel mudguards were fitted front and rear on the TSS, T140E and T140ES. Painted steel mudguards in 'burgundy' or black could be specified on the TSX. As Meriden Bonneville production drew to a close, shorter front mudguards mounted on a single central mounting bracket, as used on the later Harris Bonnevilles, were fitted.

Electrics and Speedometer

There was little change for the T140E and T140ES. The TSS came equipped with a modified form of the Lucas Rita electronic ignition timed at 30 degrees fully advanced to cater for the specialized eight-valve cylinder head. The use of Veglia instruments continued with the TSX having a revised ratio speedometer drive to adjust the calibration for the altered rolling circumference of the larger section rear tyre and 16in diameter wheel.

Seat

TSX 'low rider' was equipped with a laid back, almost reclining, seat that offered 'sit in' rather than the 'sit on' accommodation of a conventional motorcycle.

Wheels, Tyres and Brakes

Morris alloy wheels were fitted as standard on the UK T140E, whilst the more conservative US-market version retained spoked wheels. The TSX and TSS variants were fitted with Morris alloys, the TSX having 19in front and 16in rear wheels with twin rotor discs brakes as an option. All Bonnevilles had Dunlop 'All Weather' sintered metal brake pads to improve braking in the wet.

10   Bonneville Reborn

Harris Bonneville 1985

In 1985 the manufacturing plant and stock of remaining Triumph Bonneville parts were purchased by Les Harris of Racing Spares, an established component manufacturer and motorcycle spares supplier. For twenty years Racing Spares had produced parts for Norton, BSA and Triumph at its Bedfordshire factory and it was not without justification that workers at Meriden felt the Harris operation took valuable business away from their own factory. Insult was added to injury when manufacture of the complete bike fell within Harris's remit. After agreeing terms with John Bloor for a five-year production run of T140 Bonnevilles, Harris began a search for new suppliers for the specialist components required to manufacture a subtly revised Bonnie.

Significant delay was encountered due to many traditional, home-based component suppliers no longer serving the sadly depleted British motorcycle industry. Despite this, on the 25 June 1985, L.F. Harris (Rushden) Ltd was able to reproduce a slightly modified version of Triumph's final Bonneville. Although the new model's brakes were by Brembo, the forks Paioli and the instruments made by Veglia, the engine was the same old 744cc twin driving through the T140V's familiar five-speed gearbox. The twin Amal carburettors were Mark 1 Concentrics but equipped with the later Mark 2 version's cold-start arrangement. This minor revision removed a troublesome hesitancy prior to acceleration that had been present with the original Bonneville's carburettor set-up.

New Market

Since the Bonneville was introduced, road systems have changed radically. The low and mid-range torque provided by the old T120 and T140 suited the system of dual carriageways that had spanned the countryside of the 1960s and 1970s. Ease of handling allowing rapid exits from roundabouts and byway curves were the Bonneville's strengths, rather than high-speed motorway cruising. For many the characteristics built into the Bonnie retained their appeal and it was this group that formed the market for the Harris Bonneville. In spite of a modest and continuing demand for the bike in America, none could be exported due to the prohibitive expense of product liability insurance and the need for stringent safety testing of the machine to meet US import requirements.

A combination of circumstances ultimately led to the Devon Bonneville's demise. Prime cause was the suspicion that the manufacturing license would not be renewed due to the imminent opening of John Bloor's new factory at Hinckley. Marketplace conflict would have been inevitable as the two marques competed for the same customer base, albeit with very different machines. Another issue was the ever tighter legislation on noise and toxic emissions. Although the model was able to meet the regulations current at the time, the requirements could only get more onerous. As a final clincher, by early 1988 stocks of crankcase halves were running low. Production of a new batch represented a significant financial commitment to what was, in manufacturing terms,

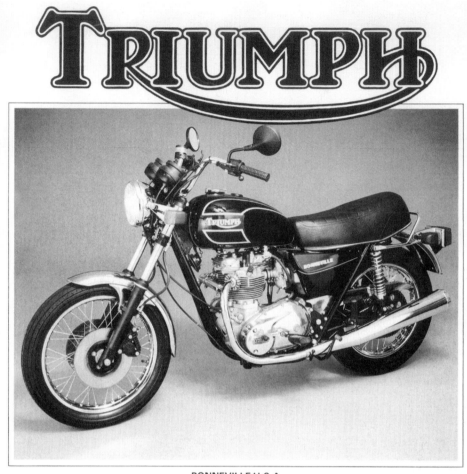

BONNEVILLE U.S.A.

Engine type: OHV parallel twin, four stroke
Bore: 76mm (2.992")
Stroke: 82mm (3.992")
Capacity: 744cc (45 cu. in.)
Compression Ratio 7.9 : 1
Carburettors: Twin Amal Mark 1.5
Tyres: Avon Roadrunner Front: F2 100/90 H19.
                Rear: 110/90 H18
Brakes: Front twin disc 260mm dia. Rear single disc
Gearbox type: five speed. Top gear 4.74
RPM at 10 mph in top gear 636

Frame: All welded steel cradle type
Hydraulic rear shock absorbers
Wheelbase: 1422mm (56")
Seat Height: 787mm (31")
Dry Weight: 186kg (410lbs) approx.
Fuel Capacity: 12.8 litre (2.8 Imp. Gallons)
Electrics: 12v crankshaft alternator, 8 A/H battery,
        contactless electronic ignition
Instruments: Tacho and Speedo
Finish: Stainless steel mudguards, Black/red flash or
        black/double gold line

The Triumph Bonneville is also made in the U.K./European specification, for details ask for leaflet No. SH85/UKB

Units 1 & 2, Silverhills Road,
Decoy Industrial Estate,
Newton Abbot,
South Devon
Telephone: 0626-69700/60486
Telex: 42902 Racing G

Produced under licence by
L.F. Harris (Rushden) Ltd.

On 25 June 1985, L.F. Harris (Rushden) Ltd. began production of a slightly modified version of the Bonneville at its workshops in Newton Abbot, Devon. In spite of a continued healthy demand for the bike in America and the designation 'Bonneville USA' beneath the brochure shot, none was exported to the US.

Rolling chassis ready for the installation of engine/gearbox units at the Harris assembly shop. Note the double disc front brake.

a very small operation. If the coup de grace had to be delivered, better it came now.

Production of the Bonneville continued at the company's workshops in Newton Abbot, Devon until the licensing agreement expired in March 1988. By that time a total of 1,255 machines had been completed.

Triumph at Hinckley: the Bonneville 2000

John Bloor had established his new Triumph company in 1984 with a staff of fourteen. Once intellectual property rights to the Triumph marque had been secured, design work on the new range of bikes began and by 1988 the

With engine and silencers fitted, this Harris Bonneville waits only for the finishing touches

company had started construction of a new factory at Dodwells Bridge Industrial Estate, Hinckley in Leicestershire.

Pre-production models were revealed to the public at the Cologne Show of 1990 and series production of the first Hinckley Triumph, the 1200cc Trophy, commenced in early 1991. By that time the staff complement had grown to 120.

The limited manufacturing agreement for the Bonneville made with Les Harris had benefited Bloor's plans by enabling the Triumph name to maintain a market presence as plans were made for the new factory. Additionally, media attention could be diverted whilst Triumph's new range of bikes was developed. As the new, modular range of multi-cylinder Triumph machines came on stream the old

Harris Bonnevilles await despatch at the Newton Abbot factory in Devon.

Bonneville was phased out. A cold, heartless, strategy maybe but, overall, commercially correct.

As in earlier years, to maximize sales of the new range, Triumph took prompt action to develop potential export markets. By 1994, as output at the Hinckley plant reached 12,000 units per year, Triumph Deutschland Gmbh, Triumph France SA and Triumph America Ltd had all been established.

Manufacturing lessons have been learned and applied to good effect in the new factory. John Burton took on the role of head of production at Hinckley and brought with him skills developed whilst running Nissan's car body shop in Washington, Tyne and Wear. Application of Nissan's Anglo-Japanese production practice has brought improved communications between management and staff so that shopfloor procedures can be analysed and

The Harris stand at the Cologne Motorcycle Show in September, 1987 only months before the expiry of the manufacturing license in March of the following year.

continuously monitored. Anybody used to the surroundings and processes of the Meriden factory would feel decidedly out of place in the muted, high-tech, production environment at Hinckley. The calm and controlled atmosphere should not be allowed to mislead visitors to the factory. Despite the hush, production levels have prospered and by mid-1996 the Hinckley factory had turned out over 40,000 new machines and annual production had reached 15,000 units per year.

Introduction of the Daytona T595 and the Speed Triple T509 at Cologne in 1996 marked a move away from the modular production philosophy employed with Triumph's initial models. Further diversification came with the release of the Sprint ST and the all new Tiger in 1998. The following year the TT600, the world's first mass-produced fuel injected 600cc sports bike, was launched.

One aspect of manufacturing at Hinckley is shared with the Meriden of the sixties: since 1991 production has been racing to keep pace with demand. Every year orders have exceeded the number of machines made. To help in that race and the all-important pursuit of a bigger market share, a larger, more modern, factory has been built with an annual production capacity of 60,000. The potential for a four-fold increase in production can often come in handy.

Hinckley Bonneville: Retro or Real?

Development of the new Bonneville started at Triumph's Hinckley factory in April 1997. For Triumph the proposed air-cooled, twin-cylinder engine represented a significant break from its range of exclusively water-cooled machines. However, popular demand for the Bonneville's reintroduction was undeniable

Same name, new century. The Triumph Bonneville produced at the Hinckley factory can readily be recognized as the machine that would have evolved; if only circumstances had allowed the original Meriden design team uninterrupted progress.

Bonneville 2000

Manufactured by John Bloor's Triumph Motorcycles Ltd (Hinckley)
Price: £5,600
Production commenced December 2000
Model: 790cc Bonneville

790cc air-cooled double overhead cam 360 degree parallel twin

Maximum power	62PS (61bhp) at 7,400rpm
Maximum torque	60 Nm (44.3ft.lb) at 3,500rpm
Bore/stroke	86 × 68mm

Twin 36mm carburettors
Compression ratio 9.2:1
Electronic ignition
Primary drive, gear driven wet, multi-plate clutch
Five-speed gearbox

Frame
Tubular steel cradle with twin-sided tubular steel swinging arm supported by twin chromed spring shock absorber units
41mm telescopic front forks
Seat height 30.5in

Fuel tank

Capacity	16 litres (4.3 gallons US); approximate range at 54mpg, 190 miles (300km)

Wheels and tyres

Front wheel	19 × 2.5 spoked, with 100/90 × 19 Bridgestone tyre
Rear wheel	17 × 3.5 spoked, with 130/80 × 17 Bridgestone tyre

Brakes

Front	Single 310mm disc with two-piston caliper
Rear	Single 255mm disc with two-piston caliper

---

and by July 1997 the concept had been outlined and finance for the project allocated. By March 1999 the 790cc power unit was running in a prototype chassis.

The design brief specified a machine with the appeal and styling of the late sixties version of the T120 Bonneville, possessing the power and practicality needed for modern use. To this end considerable effort was made to reproduce the essential appearance of the sixties bike with effective, but discreetly applied, hi-tech engineering solutions to the original bike's long-standing design problems.

Slight conflict existed in that some of those early design problems had become well-loved features of the T120 Bonneville. Whilst the reborn Bonneville's twin balancers reduce engine vibration at the top end of the rev range, Hinckley has taken care to retain an element of the living, sensuous, vibes that characterized the T120 Bonnie. Retro-looking, pea-shooter type silencers have been upgraded to meet current exhaust emissions with the application of a modern-day air injection system, and the old push rod valve gear has been replaced by four valves per cylinder operated by double overhead camshafts. The camshafts are driven by a chain routed between the cylinders. What might look like the good old T120's exhaust valve push rod tube is in fact an oil drain for the carefully concealed oil cooler that nestles discretely beneath the fuel tank. Twin 36mm carburettors feature throttle position sensors and electric heater elements to ease starting and prevent induction icing.

One, almost essential, retro-chic feature has been omitted: the kick-start option.

Rider's Report

For me, the initial disappointment at not finding a kick-starter quickly faded when road test time came. What had been the all too easy, electric start soft option soon became accepted as the only option. Fuel on, pull out the choke mounted on the left-hand carb, restore the kill switch and press the electric starter button. Smoothly and without drama the motor rolled into life; simultaneously this born-again Bonneville became a taut and living creature.

First gear engaged with a gentle crunch so familiar that it was impossible not to connect with the many earlier journeys made on many earlier Triumphs. The drive was taken up smoothly as the light, progressive, clutch was released and power applied. With no rev counter to monitor, power can be applied in a relaxed style or with more vigour using the muted engine roar to indicate gear change intervals. Either way, there is no need for frenetic use of rpm as maximum torque is produced at a modest 3,500rpm, and with 90 per cent of that maximum available at just 2,750rpm, engine flexibility features prominently.

On the road, gear swap intervals are clearly indicated by the subdued engine note as the rpm increase. A second, perhaps more generous, bite can be taken out of the power curve as the next ratio is engaged. This process is repeated up through the five-speed 'box with each satisfactory surge of power being delivered in a smooth and precisely defined manner.

Apart from the obvious changes in power output and fittings, evidence of the Hinckley Bonneville's Triumph genealogy is startling. The machine's lineage is apparent even in the ride characteristics. The bike retains the charm and good looks of the original Bonneville, tastefully combined with current standards of equipment and the performance essential for fast and prolonged modern-day travel. Around town the Bonnie can be so accurately posi-tioned that slow-speed manoeuvring through standing traffic becomes a pleasure. Purposeful and predictable at all speeds, the Bonneville's handling on the open road makes it a stable and secure platform from which to plan safe routes past slower traffic, with the bike's reliable per-formance ensuring a more than adequate response when those plans are executed.

Switch gear and minor controls are well thought out and easily operated with a gloved hand, allowing total concentration to be focused on the road ahead. The 'head up' riding position enables a wide field of vision to be comfortably maintained, although the view to the rear through the round, convex driving mirrors is slightly restricted. Perhaps the mirrors were partly screened by my own, some might say excessively, wide bulk, but I maintain that the restricted field of rear vision is mainly due to the narrow spread of the mirror mount-ing stalks.

The 790cc Hinckley Bonneville can readily be recognized as the machine that would have evolved if only commercial circumstances had allowed the original Meriden design team uninterrupted progress. In the same way that the Meriden T120 was ideally suited to the environment of its day, the dual carriageways and leafy byroads of a bygone Britain, so the Hinckley Bonneville has been tailored to the urban travel of the modern day.

11   Conclusion

Ultimately the seeds of failure for the British motorcycle industry could be seen in the fruits of its success. Edward Turner's designs resulted in inspired products bringing justified recognition and early rewards to the Triumph company. Subsequent development was carried out single-mindedly to the detriment of alternative avenues of research. Although easily identified in retrospect, this static design policy, born of complacency, ultimately proved commercially fatal for the company and industry alike.

The introduction of the Speed Twin in 1937 was a revelation. The machine was fast, smooth and modern, clearly a generation removed from the lack-lustre competition of the day. Early development followed but, possibly due to Turner's autocratic manner, coherent long-term research for future products exploiting technological advance was not undertaken. Before the omission was realized, time and money were running out for Triumph. The company was forced to work with the engine it had, matching the genuine innovative advances of the competition by repeatedly increasing the capacity and heightening the state of tune of its own outdated design. Inevitably, reliability suffered.

Even when pressed into a policy shift, as with the Triumph Trident, management inertia blunted the edge of progress. By trading on the Bonneville's past success, Trident might have been given an initial market boost. Without Turner's reluctance the three-cylinder ohv Trident could have been brought to market in 1964–65. Delays and compromise resulting from committee-based decision-making further hindered the Trident's introduction, and when the model was eventually released in the late summer

of 1968 it received only partial success. Not until it was restyled for the 1971 season did the bike become fully accepted by the paying customer.

The Trident's cylinder dimensions, gearbox and many ancillaries were taken directly from Triumph's good old, same old, 500/650/750cc twins and serve to illustrate the stagnation of design within the company. Additionally, Trident's equipment specification was unattractively low relative to other bikes readily available on the market at the time. No electric starter, no fifth gear and modest drum brakes, even though at the front in effective twin-leading-shoe form. In spite of all this and the bike's late release with an already outdated ohv spec, the Trident did achieve significant sporting success and managed reasonable sales. However, the delayed introduction gave other contenders, notably the Japanese, a crucial advantage which they exploited to the full. Managed properly and introduced promptly the Trident could have given so much more, so much earlier; perhaps even providing an escape route from the downward financial spiral that the company later followed.

The same management that delayed the introduction of the Trident perversely advocated BSA's parallel production of the Rocket 3, another three-cylinder machine. Not a badge-engineered replica of the Trident, instead the same package aimed at the same customer, produced by the same manufacturing group with expensive, fundamental differences in both styling and engineering.

In July 1970 came the Ariel 3, a very unusual 50cc moped with a pivoted frame that allowed the front to bank over for a bend whilst both the twin rear wheels stayed in contact with the road.

Management claimed to have been misled by flawed market research, but either way, this unpopular machine ultimately cost the company £2m at a time when funds were fast running out. Mistakes of this order could not be repeated.

Lack of decision, a willingness to stay with the conventional or a perverse readiness to embrace the outlandish, all symptoms of approaching failure that can be readily identified in retrospect. The final demise of NVT, fatally undermined by the Meriden sit-in, marked the end of any hope for a viable British motorcycle industry.

Appendix I
Identification

The frame number for all Bonnevilles is found on the left-hand side of the frame downtube, just below the steering head. The alpha-numeric code for early Bonnies takes the form of a date-code prefix letter followed by a six-figure frame number. Engine numbers matched the frame number when bikes left the factory, although over time many machines were modified with engines, and numbered crankcases, often being swapped with little regard to numbering scheme continuity. In 1960 the Duplex frames were given a D prefix and the numbering scheme started with 101. This system was maintained until 1962.

When unit construction of engine and gearbox started in 1963 the prefix DU was used and the numbers restarted from 101. The whole system was revised in 1969 when two code letters denoting month and year of manufacture were applied.

Engine number prefix letters, 1969–80

First letter	Month of manufacture	Second letter	Year of manufacture
A	January	C	1969
B	February	D	1970
C	March	E	1971
D	April	G	1972
E	May	H	1973
G	June	J	1974
H	July	K	1975
J	August	N	1976
K	September	P	1977
N	October	X	1978
P	November	A	1979
X	December	B	1980

For the period 1981–83 a three-letter code was used to denote the year of manufacture: KDA = 1981, EDA = 1982, BEA = 1983.

The model year started in the August of the preceding calendar year as the factory's annual holidays finished and workers started manufacturing stock for the coming season.

The engine number suffix letter indicates the machine's original description and technical features.

Engine suffix letters 1959–83

Suffix letter	Model description	Manufacture
No suffix	UK road	1959
A	US road	1960
B	US street scrambler	1960
R	US road	Post 1960
C	US street scramble	Post 1960
TT	US TT special	1966–67
RT	US 750cc	1970
V	Five speed	Post 1973
E	Reduced emissions	Post 1978
ES	Electric start	Post 1980
D	Special	1979–80
AV	Anti-vibration (police)	1981
LE	Limited edition, Royal	1982
TSS	Eight-valve	1983
TSX	Low rider custom	1983

Appendix II
Significant Technical Changes During the Bonneville's Production

1959
Introduced with nacelle-mounted headlamp and instruments. 'Chopped' Amal Monobloc carburettors with central, remotely mounted Amal float chamber. Separate engine and gearbox with magneto ignition and manual advance lever.

1960
Duplex frame introduced. Separate chromed headlamp shell. Black seat with white piping. Crankshaft mounted alternator and magneto ignition with automatic advance. Float chamber mounted on engine cylinder head steady to reduce frothing. US off-road competition variants released.

1961
Duplex frame strengthened by the addition of a lower tank rail. Standard 'unchopped' Monobloc carbs with integral float bowls. Improved anti-vibration rubber insulation for the three-point fuel tank mounting. Anti-vibration brackets for oil tank. 18in rear wheel. Fully floating brake shoes front and rear.

1962
Two-tone slate on grey seat upholstery separated by white piping. Smiths Chronometric speedometer reads up to 140mph.

1963
Unit construction engine and gearbox with nine-stud head. Contact breaker points mounted in engine timing cover control coils fitted underneath petrol tank. Single downtube frame, 18in front wheel.

1964
Smiths 125mph magnetic speedo replaces Chronometric. TT Special released onto the US market.

1965
Thicker fuel tank rubber knee grips. Fork stanchions 1in longer and lighter external springs fitted.

1966
Full-width hub at the front. Slimmer fuel tank with new badges. Steering lock improved by modifying bottom yoke. Steering head angle revised to 62 degrees from previous 65 degrees. New rear brake drum. Tank-mounted parcel rack deleted for US market.

1967
Smiths speedometer reads to 150mph. Quilted seat cover, grey with black sides. Final year for the US TT special.

1968
Amal Concentric carburettors replace Monoblocs. Twelve-point cylinder base mounting nuts. Stronger swinging arm. Shuttle valve damping for front forks. Independently adjustable contact breaker points. Standard air filters. Improved upholstery available in two-tone grey or black on hinged seat.

1969

Parcel rack deleted. Nitrided camshafts, heavier crankshaft and flywheel. Thinner knee grips and revised tank badges on new fuel tank. Triumph logo background for engine number to improve security. Balanced exhaust system. Passenger grab-rail. Wider forks allow fitting of a larger-section front tyre.

1970

Windtone horns, adjustable pre-load on rear shock absorber units. Grab-rail mounted on sub-frame.

1971

Oil-in-frame chassis. New forks featuring internal springs, hard chromed stanchions with alloy sliders. Front-wheel spindle secured by four bolt spindle clamps on each side. Chrome wire brackets support headlamp. Squarer 'breadbin' tank for UK models. Conical wheel hubs at front and rear with twin leading shoe front brake. Direction indicators made standard equipment. Matched, rubber-mounted speedometer and tachometer. Along with the new frame came a new seat, chainguard, engine plates, mudguards and megaphone exhausts.

1972

T120V five-speed model introduced and marketed alongside four-speed version. Frame lowered and seat thinned to reduce overall height. Extra front mudguard stay. Cylinder head revised for push in exhaust fitment.

1973

724cc T140 launched and soon uprated top 744cc. Ten-bolt cylinder head, chrome-plated mudguards, 10in disc brake. Ignition switch shifted from left-side panel to left fork shroud. New fork to allow fitment of front disc brake.

1974

Improved silencers with reverse taper end section were fitted before production of the 1974 model was interrupted by industrial action in October 1973.

1975

650cc T120 dropped from Triumph range. Blockaded stock 1974 machines released to dealers.

1976

A new hydraulic rear disc brake and the major switch to left foot gear change dictate substantial alteration to frame and primary drive cover.

1977

Limited edition Jubilee Bonneville has extra chrome with a red, blue and silver paint job.

1978

Veglia instruments introduced to Triumph range. Cleaner running T140E launched with closed-circuit engine breathing. Chromed upper fork shrouds fitted.

1979

Amal Mark II carburettors made standard and cylinder head revised to suit. T140D with alloy Lester wheels and stepped seat launched. Knee-grips deleted. Three-phase charging system and negative earth electrics installed.

1980

Starter motor fitted to the newly launched T140ES requires modifications to the timing cover. T140D-style mounting of the rear brake calliper, i.e. above the swinging arm, is made standard on all machines. All models are fitted with Veglia instruments.

1981

Executive model is introduced featuring twin front discs, colour-coded fairing and matching luggage as standard. Morris alloy wheels standard fitment on Executive and T140D Special.

1982

New fuel tank with flip-up filler cap. Twin disc front brake set up made available as option on all models. Square-section direction indicators manufactured in black plastic. Executive and all US models fitted with Marzocchi rear suspension and Bing CV carburettors.

1983

TSS and its eight-valve head leads the Triumph Bonneville range into its final year. The custom styled TSX has a 16in rear wheel carrying fat-section rear tyre, short silencers and painted mudguards. Laid-back style emphasized by low seat height and high handlebars. Spoked wheels remain standard for the US.

Index